THE
COFFEE
BOOK

THE COFFEE BOOK

A Connoisseur's Guide to Gourmet Coffee

JOHN SVICAROVICH
STEPHEN WINTER
JEFF FERGUSON

Drawings by Lauren Rosen

PRENTICE-HALL, INC.
ENGLEWOOD CLIFFS, N.J.

To those who
love the savor of
truly good coffee

THE COFFEE BOOK: A *Connoisseur's Guide to Gourmet Coffee*
by John Svicarovich, Stephen Winter and Jeff Ferguson

Copyright © 1976 by John Svicarovich, Stephen Winter and Jeff Ferguson

Printed in the United States of America

Prentice-Hall International, Inc., London
Prentice-Hall of Australia, Pty. Ltd., Sydney
Prentice-Hall of Canada, Ltd., Toronto
Prentice-Hall of India Private Ltd., New Delhi
Prentice-Hall of Japan, Inc., Tokyo
10 9 8 7 6 5 4 3 2 1

Library of Congress Cataloging in Publication Data

Svicarovich, John
The coffee book.

1. Coffee. I. Winter, Stephen, joint author.
II. Ferguson, Jeff, joint author.
III. Title.
TX817. C6S9   641.8'77   75-37820
ISBN 0-13-139675-7

ACKNOWLEDGMENTS

We are grateful to the following people for their help in verifying and expanding upon information used in various parts of this book: John Adinolfi, director, Coffee Brewing Center of the Pan-American Coffee Bureau; his colleague Bob Thomas and all the other people at both the Coffee Brewing Center and the parent Pan-American Coffee Bureau in New York City; Michael Sivetz, coffee processing consultant, Corvallis, Oregon; Erna K. Guerrieri, gourmet coffee specialist, B.C. Ireland, Inc., San Francisco; the Coffee Industry Board of Jamaica and its general manager, F.A. Briscoe; Milton Montgomery, gourmet coffee specialist, United Coffee Corporation, San Francisco; Don Hoffler, owner of Windward Trading Company, Mill Valley, California; Dr. Michael Toren, cardiologist and gourmet, Portland, Oregon; and Dr. John Nastro, specialist in pulmonary medicine, Los Angeles.

Thanks also to the Pan-American Coffee Bureau for permission to use its cold coffee drink and coffee cooking recipes; to Candy Withycombe, Portland, Oregon, for research assistance; and to Jackie Bobzien, Portland, Oregon, for typing the manuscript.

Published resources used in the preparation of this book include *All About Coffee*, by William H. Ukers; *Coffee*, an abstract by Michael Sivetz; *Coffee: Botany, Cultivation and Utilization*, by Frederick L. Wellman; *Coffee Processing Technology*, by Michael Sivetz; *The Pharmacological Basis of Therapeutics*, by Louis S. Goodman and Alfred Gilman; "Coffee and Cardiovascular Disease," by Dr. Thomas R. Dawber and colleagues, *The New England Journal of Medicine*, October 24, 1974; "Coffee Drinking and Acute Myocardial Infarction," by Dr. Hershel Jick and colleagues, *The Lancet*, December 16, 1972; "Coffee and Myocardial Infarction," by Dr. Jick and colleagues, *The New England Journal of Medicine*, July 12, 1973; "Coffee Drinking Prior to Acute Myocardial Infarction," by Dr. Arthur L. Klatsky and colleagues, *Journal of the American Medical Association*, October 29, 1973; "Coffee and Its Physiological Effects," by Dr. G. Czok, Physiologisch-Chemisches Institut der Universität, Mainz (translated from German); "Coronary Heart Disease and Caffeine," a reference paper from the Coffee Information Institute, New York City; "A Longitudinal Study of Coronary Heart Disease," by Dr. Oglesby Paul and colleagues, *Circulation*, July 1973; and "Stimulants and Coronaries," by Dr. Paul, *Postgraduate Medicine*, September 1968.

CONTENTS

THE
COFFEE
BOOK

1.
COMING BACK TO GOOD COFFEE

A good cup of coffee has to be one of the greatest of those small pleasures in life, adding with its warmth, flavor, and aroma a bit of uplift and a common touch-point for sharing time with a friend. Good whole-bean coffee and good ways to brew it are very old, so their growing popularity the past few years represents a rediscovery—part of a larger return to many fine old things. Yet to each person the discovery of good coffee presents a whole new world. The idea of this book is to help you explore and enjoy that world.

Even though it is often called gourmet or special-ty coffee to distinguish it from the mass market coffees on the grocery store shelf, good coffee is readily acces-sible to the consumer who seeks it out. It not only offers a wide variety of flavors that can be enjoyed every day, it costs only about five cents a cup.

We know from our own experience that most people who discover good coffee may be a bit overwhelmed at first by its diversity and technical side. The whole bean coffee store is intimidating enough by itself. It may contain as many as a dozen of the world's best coffees, several special roasts and blends, half a dozen grinders, just as many different brewers, and a broad assortment of accessories. Then there is buying, storing, grinding, and brewing. These steps to good coffee are not mysterious or difficult, but they do require some fundamental knowledge and care.

In view of renewed consumer interest in good coffee and all the specialty coffee stores opening around the country, we were concerned that there existed no reliable, consumer-oriented guide to enjoying good coffee. Some small paperbacks claiming to represent the consumer's interest have been published, but they contain a rather superficial treatment of coffee buying and preparation, as well as a lot of inaccuracies, much useless trivia, and in one case a self-indulgence characteristic of vanity-press writing. Serious works on coffee by authorities like Ukers and Wellman are too technical and not at all designed to help the consumer with such questions as how to judge the quality of roast beans, buy a grinder, choose a brewing system, and experiment with blending.

One Oregon spring evening, over some exquisite cups of Ethiopia Harrar, we decided to write such a book. We did so with the conviction that what we had learned in the discovery and enjoyment of good coffee would be useful to others interested in the same rewarding experience. As a frame of reference for what we thought was needed, we decided to write the book we'd like to have had when we first began to enjoy specialty coffees. What we offer is some practical lore that we've come to know through the hard route of asking our own questions as consumers, spending our own money on coffee and coffee paraphernalia, experimenting on our own time, and finding both success and failure in our efforts. Where we weren't sure about something, we did consult more knowledgeable sources. If they didn't agree with one another, or if we didn't agree with them, we generally relied on our own judgment. Although we are grateful to coffee experts for their help, we were mindful that none of them had managed, in modern times, to produce a single useful book for coffee consumers, even though they all agree that one was needed years ago.

Inside the Coffee Book

Following this introduction, the book begins by characterizing quality coffee and describing some of the world's premium coffees available in the United States and Canada. Then it goes on to tell you how you can judge the quality of roast beans in your local coffee store. It discusses the principles of grinding and brewing, and it gives evaluative descriptions of the grinding and brewing systems that are available. It outlines the principles and techniques of blending, and then suggests some blends, some hot and cold coffee drinks, and some coffee cooking recipes you might like to try. It reviews medical findings on coffee's effects on health and points out how you can enjoy good coffee even if you want to cut your caffeine intake. For those who are interested, it moves on to describe coffee growing and processing, and how they affect coffee quality.

For some it may seem odd that there's no section on coffee history, and that coffee growing and processing is at the back of the book. A certain kind of logic dictates that one should begin with history, describe growing and processing, and then move on to roasting, marketing, buying, and so forth. The problem with this kind of approach is that it doesn't get around very quickly to helping you learn what you need to know as a coffee consumer. It follows the coffee bean's journey to you, not your journey to good coffee. So we're beginning with the focus on what you probably want to know initially. Although there's no section on history, we do include historical information from time to time to illustrate various points. A rundown on growing and processing belongs in the book because these segments of the coffee business affect the quality of the coffee you have to buy. The chapter on growing and processing will give you a better understanding of the overall coffee trade. However, we've put it in the back because it doesn't tell you anything you need to know immediately to begin buying and enjoying good coffee.

As far as we know, this is the first book on gourmet coffee that discusses the inferiority of mass market coffee. Because the world coffee trade is a $4 billion annual business and because the big mass market coffee concerns have a dominant role in it, they have long held sway over the public's understanding of coffee. For example, the three major mass market coffee concerns in the United States control more than 60 percent of the market, exceed $1 billion in annual sales, and spend about $40 million a year on advertising. Although the mass market concerns have filled a need for cheap, tolerable coffee, they also have played a major role in creating that need through their enormous dominance of the marketplace and their influence over the public's coffee knowledge and coffee-drinking habits.

Like thousands of other coffee drinkers who have broken away from that influence, we have found specialty coffee not only delicious to savor but exciting to explore. We wish you the same rewards, and, at the same time, hope this book will make them easier to come by.

2.

A TRUE TASTER'S CHOICE

The growing coffee specialty business presents you with a lot of tantalizing choices in coffee taste. Most whole bean coffee stores carry at least a dozen different coffees from around the world. However, these choices can seem overwhelming if you are just getting acquainted with good coffee. The purpose of this chapter is to look at the nature of gourmet coffee, to see how it differs from mass market coffee, and to discuss some of the main flavor varieties and roasts available in any good coffee store.

WHAT GOURMET COFFEE IS

Without exception, gourmet or specialty coffee comes from high-grade Arabica beans. Arabica, pronounced air-a-BEE-ca, is the world's most important species of coffee, both in taste and commercial value. Properly roasted and brewed, good Arabica beans make a fragrant, delicious cup of coffee. Although Arabicas make up three-fourths of the world coffee market and are blended into mass market coffee, the best of them are generally not available except in whole bean form in quality coffee stores. The best Arabicas are usually grown at high altitudes in nitrogen-rich soils. They are hand-picked at the moment of ripeness, carefully cleaned and dried, and then sorted for quality (see Chapter 8).

Until modern times, the history of coffee is virtually the history of Arabica coffee. The Arabica plant was first cultivated in Ethiopia sometime before A.D. 600, after someone discovered that the dried, roasted, and ground seeds of its cherrylike fruit made a pleasant tasting brew which brought on a good feeling and mental alertness. Sometime thereafter, the plant was adopted by the Arabian culture from which it derives its name. The drug properties of this *cahoueh*, as the beverage was known, created quite a stir in the world of Islam, forming battle lines between prohibitionists and defenders of the drink. But by the 1500s the beverage was firmly entrenched in Middle Eastern religion, customs, and diet. By the late 1600s, coffee had caught on in Europe, especially among the leisured and influential classes. A French courtesan of that day properly called it "the new drug," and even from our distant vantage point, we can see that coffee's stimulating effects must have made it fashionable and daring before it became practical. Soon coffee became very popular, and to meet the growing market for it, European powers (especially the French and the

Dutch) began to introduce Arabica plants into the tropical regions they were eagerly conquering and exploiting. This was fairly easy to do because the plant is self-pollinating, very fertile, and able to grow under a variety of conditions.

People who love good coffee may be surprised to discover the debt they owe to Louis XIV of France. Most of the Arabicas in the world directly descend from a plant of Ethiopian origin given to him by the Dutch in 1713. The monarch, a coffee connoisseur who shrewdly assessed the market value of the beverage, ordered his five-foot tree carefully tended for propagation. Then he had its seedlings sent to France's far-flung colonies, where they were successfully cultivated. Not long after, descendants of those seedlings were being cultivated in other French, Spanish, Dutch, Portuguese, and British tropical holdings. The result today is billions of Arabica plants around the world, all from that one royal forebear.

Because of genetic mutation, selective propagation, and different growing conditions, the descendants of Louis's original plant have a number of pleasing taste variations. Chief Arabica regions today include tropical zones of the Western Hemisphere, Africa and Arabia, and southern Asia between the Indian and Pacific oceans. Brazil is currently the leading export country in the world, with Colombia ranking second. Other countries important in the production of Arabica coffee include Mexico, Venezuela, Ethiopia, Kenya, Indonesia, and most of the Central American nations. The United States produces the unique Kona variety of Arabica in Hawaii.

WHAT GOURMET COFFEE ISN'T

Although the focus of this book is gourmet coffee, we believe it's important to distinguish it from the mass-produced coffees that still dominate the marketplace. Gourmet and mass market coffees differ not only in taste, content, and price, but also in the flavor options they present to the consumer, the control the consumer can exercise over their freshness, and the ways in which they are marketed.

In the final analysis, taste is the most important difference between specialty and mass market coffee. High-grown beans that are harvested and processed with great care make a better-tasting cup of coffee than other beans that aren't. Mass market coffees don't taste as good as gourmet coffees because they contain inferior ingredients: lower-grade Arabicas, Robusta beans, and, in some cases, adulterates like chicory. In addition, mass market coffees are neither roasted nor stored with the care of high-grade coffees. Their price, which is 40 to 50 percent lower than specialty coffees, reflects that difference.

Robusta is the only coffee species of significance besides Arabica, and because it has such a prominent role in the inferior (and declining) quality of mass market coffee, it deserves some brief attention. Robusta coffee has a decidedly unpleasant taste, but since its commercial introduction in the 1900s, the Robusta plant has proved economically attractive to many coffee growers because of its resistance to disease, its adaptability and hardiness, its ease of harvesting, and its average yield of 700 pounds of clean beans per acre compared to an average Arabica yield of 300 pounds per acre. These factors have made Robustas cheap and attractive to mass coffee processors.

Most Robusta beans come from Africa, but some are also grown in parts of India, Indonesia, and Latin America. They are smaller than most Arabica beans and more rounded and irregular in shape. The only Arabicas similar in appearance to Robusta are "pea" beans like Tanzania. However, that's where the resemblance ends. Candid coffee experts have likened Robusta coffee's taste to that of burned rubber and its aroma to that of urine. No self-respecting or survival-oriented whole bean coffee store would sell Robusta beans, but their use in mass market coffee is on the increase.

At this writing, the most recent statistics of the Pan-American Coffee Bureau show that U.S. imports of Robusta beans have steadily increased from 9.1 percent in 1959 to a high of 31.9 percent in 1974. Interestingly enough, the Bureau's statistics show per capita coffee consumption in the United States declining from a high of 3.12 cups per day in 1962 to 2.25 cups in 1974.

Since Robusta beans produce a sour cup of coffee, even when skillfully treated or blended, it is difficult to avoid the inference that increased use of Robusta in the mass coffee market has been an important factor in declining coffee consumption.

As we discuss in the next section of this chapter, gourmet coffees offer the consumer a world of flavor options. However, most mass market coffee is sold simply as "coffee." Some of the better canned coffees might declare the country or countries of origin, but they don't offer information on bean type or grade. Most mass market coffee is blended, and the manufacturers refuse to reveal the ingredients, claiming the privilege to retain "trade secrets." But because mass market blending is used to hide bad flavors as much as highlight good ones, this claim of privilege appears to be designed partly to keep the consumer unaware of the kinds of mediocre coffees behind the label. In view of the vast amount of mass market coffee consumed, it's remarkable that the industry is not required by law to declare the bean types, grades, and blend ratios of its coffees.

Mass market coffees also differ from whole bean specialty coffees in freshness and in the capacity to keep fresh. As we note in the next chapter, you can personally determine and control the freshness of whole bean specialty coffee. People in the coffee trade tell us that even vacuum packing permits some degree of staling in ground coffee, although it's probably not significant. What is significant about ground, vacuum-packed coffee is that it's vulnerable to staling within hours once the can is open.

Finally, to wrap up the comparison, gourmet and mass market coffees are marketed by wholly different methods. For the most part, whole bean coffee stores have a relatively low-key approach to selling their product. They usually rely on a favorable business location and the growing awareness among a largely younger clientele that excellent coffee is not only available, but routinely so. They label the origin and character of their coffee beans clearly, and the con-

sumer can personally examine them to determine
their quality and freshness. Such shops frequently lo-
cate in shopping centers and renovated old buildings
that feature products which are either handcrafted,
imported, or of a very high quality. There, the coffee
merchant often also sells such items as teas, spices, ice
cream, chocolates, and kitchen utensils.

Mass market coffee concerns, on the other hand,
rely heavily on mass-media advertising and grocery
outlets to move their products. Since their coffee has
no particular merit other than low price, these
businesses push millions of dollars into advertising
high in emotional appeal, devoid of factual information about the coffee's content, and rash in the claims
to quality. The advertising is frequently sexist and
nearly always inane—produced with a lack of taste
and a lack of respect for the consumer that matches
the coffee being promoted.

TASTES FROM AROUND THE WORLD

If we've discovered anything about the tastes of
Arabica coffees from our reading, talks with coffee
people, and our own experiments, it's that no two
people describe them the same way. We've tasted
enough coffee to fill a small swimming pool, and even
when the three of us have carried out our tasting experiments together, we haven't arrived at complete
descriptive agreement.

So, rather than doing a coffee-by-coffee description or a taste chart, we're going to give you enough of

a general description of available Arabicas so you can take off on your own journey through the world of good coffee experiences. We believe the only description of any value is the one delivered by your own senses. And besides, the discovery is at least half the fun.

Coffee Names

Before looking at the different coffees available, we should take a moment to discuss the way beans are named. Gourmet coffees are always identified first by the country where they are grown. Thus, Kenya will be labeled "Kenya" and Colombia, "Colombia." However, a more descriptive term is often appended to the label. For example, "Harrar" in Ethiopia refers to the region of Ethiopia where this quality coffee originates. Colombia "Supremo" refers to Colombia's best grade of large, high grown, hand-picked beans as distinguished from Colombia "Excelso," a grade which is less perfect and somewhat smaller. If you're not sure about the type of coffee indicated by the extra descriptive term, ask the coffee retailer. The extra term may refer to the region where the coffee is grown, the genetic strain of the crop, the grade, or even the particular flavor character.

American Coffees

We're grouping all coffees grown in the Western Hemisphere under this heading. Major producers include Brazil, Colombia, Mexico, Guatemala, Honduras, El Salvador, Nicaragua, Costa Rica, Venezuela, Ecuador, Peru, Haiti, and the Dominican Republic.

On the whole, these countries export high-quality beans which are usually best roasted light to medium. These coffees are excellent for breakfast or midday drinking. If you're just starting to drink good coffee, these are the ones to begin with. They are roasted about the same degree as the mild mass market coffees, so they won't be a shock to your senses like some of the darker roasts.

American coffees are generally mild with a slightly acidic, tangy nip to them. These coffees are also very aromatic, so you'll enjoy them on your palate as well as your tongue.

Jamaica Blue Mountain and Kona are two American coffees which deserve special mention. The island of Jamaica plays a minor role in world coffee commerce, but it does grow what is generally acknowledged to be the ambrosia of coffees, Jamaica Blue Mountain. Extremely mellow and aromatic, this most desired of coffees is grown in ideal conditions on just a few plantations in the Blue Mountain region of the island.

For years Japan has enjoyed a near monopoly on the Jamaica coffee crop, including the high-grown Blue Mountain. However, about 10,000 pounds of Blue Mountain do enter the United States yearly. On the West Coast, Jamaica Blue Mountain is available only from stores with wholesale connections to B.C. Ireland, a San Francisco importer which receives roughly half of the U.S. supply; on the East Coast it is available only at Zabar's Gourmet Foods, a New York

City store which imports the other half, and which also carries the only Jamaica High Mountain Supreme available in the United States.

Although 10,000 pounds is a very small amount of coffee, even in the gourmet trade, some whole bean shops, particularly in the East, are defrauding customers with a seemingly endless supply of what they purport to be Jamaica Blue Mountain. Some of these stores claim they managed to get some Blue Mountain through European sources, but these claims are a bit lame and backed by questionable documentation. The Coffee Industry Board of Jamaica, which carefully controls its exports, flatly refutes the availability of Jamaica Blue Mountain to any U.S. sources other than the two mentioned here.

Kona is more available in the United States than Blue Mountain, but there is a lot less of it around than other good coffees. It's also more expensive than most other coffees, partly because of its limited availability and partly because it is a U.S. commodity involving higher labor costs than foreign coffee. Grown in the volcanic soil of Kona, Hawaii, this coffee is thin in body and sharp on the tongue, with a hint of a nutty flavor. Kona beans are large, perfectly shaped, and uniform in color. Some coffee connoisseurs dismiss Kona as harsh, but others enjoy its distinctive flavor either for brewing alone or for blending.

African and Arabian Coffees

Although Africa produces most of the Robusta beans used as filler in mass market coffee, it also exports

some good Arabicas. Major African exporters of
Arabica coffees include Kenya, Ethiopia, Nigeria,
Tanzania, Burundi, and the Ivory Coast. Yemen pro-
duces Arabian Mocha.

The coffees of this part of the world, roasted
medium to medium dark, have a good aroma and a
pleasing dry taste. Many consumers like the subtle,
cocoalike flavor in Mocha and some of the northern-
grown Africans. Both Africans and Arabians make excellent after-dinner or leisurely luncheon coffees. One
thing to be aware of in some African and Arabian coffees is the frequent mixture of high- and low-grade
beans. U. S. buyers do import some high-grade coffees
from this part of the world, such as Kenya AA. However, some Ethiopia and some Mocha is sold in the
United States in mixed grades. These coffees are still
relatively good; they just aren't as good as some of the
coffees these countries sell to other customers such as
the Europeans.

Indonesian Coffees

Indonesian coffees are the only Asian-grown Arabicas
which can be found in significant quantities in coffee
specialty shops in the United States. Indonesian coffees are grown in four of the principal islands of the
East Indies: Sumatra, Java, Celebes, and New
Guinea. Both Celebes and Sumatra make excellent
after-dinner coffees. They are characterized by full
aroma and body and a deep mellow flavor that lingers
long after the coffee is gone. Properly roasted Celebes
(medium dark) makes an intoxicating cup of coffee.

Java and New Guinea tend to be thin, dry, and slightly sour in taste. They are generally available in medium to medium-light roasts, although New Guinea is usually roasted slightly lighter than Java. These coffees are considerably milder than most of the world's Arabicas, but are somewhat shallow as well.

ROASTS AND ROASTING

With most coffees, the purpose of roasting is to bring out the flavor potential within the green bean. Air close to 400° F. is forced through the beans as rapidly as possible so that they first dry and then roast. The heat breaks down the cellular structure of the beans, causing chemical changes which liberate the oils and gases that give coffee its flavor and aroma. The person operating the roaster is guided by temperature, roasting time, changes in bean color, and personal experience in determining when beans have reached their peak flavor. As a rule, lighter roasted beans are usually smaller and denser, and their sharp or tangy flavor characteristics are enhanced. By contrast, darker roasting produces a slightly larger bean characterized by a deeper, mellower flavor.

Since each experienced roaster has a particular notion of peak flavor development for each kind of bean, there is some variance in the way coffees are roasted. Although most coffee merchants roast the same type of beans to the same general degree, you will find some differences among coffee shops. As we point out in the next chapter, this will probably affect your whole bean buying practices. For example, although most specialty shops market a light Colombia, some also offer a dark Colombia roast. Some roasters (and consumers) also favor a fairly dark roast in some of the richer coffees like Celebes Kalossi and Sumatra Mandehling.

The Dark Roasts

There are several coffees in which the roast itself dictates the flavor, and the inherent taste characteristics of the bean are less important. These are the dark roasts such as French, espresso, and Vienna. These traditional dark roasts, all of European origin, are achieved by roasting the beans to the verge of charring. Thus the roast dominates the flavor of the beans. These roasts vary in degree. Theoretically, French roast is the darkest of the dark roasts. In the roaster, it should be taken to the point at which it is ready to catch fire. In practice, however, Italian or espresso is generally the darkest roast on the market and French roast is slightly lighter. Vienna roast is not quite as dark as espresso or French. There is a so-called continental roast sometimes offered in specialty shops. However, this is a loose term for a dark European roast, and it seems to have more value as a marketing gimmick than as a definition of roast degree.

As a rule, premium beans are not used for dark roasts since their delicate values would be sacrificed to no particular avail.

Roasting Your Own Beans

If you live near a good coffee store or have mail-order access to fresh roasted beans, there's no advantage in roasting your own beans. Roasting is an art that demands study, practice, and quality equipment. Even though home-sized electric roasters are available for purchase in some coffee stores, and though it's possible to roast beans with your own kitchen equipment, the extra labor of home roasting is still not likely to give you beans roasted any better than what you can buy.

However, if you're a fierce do-it-yourselfer or summer exile in a forest lookout tower, you may want to give it a try. Just don't say we didn't warn you.

With a regular kitchen range, the two simplest methods are to shake the beans in a frying pan over a burner or to bake them slowly in the oven. Either method is usually inferior to commercial roasting because you have no way of *forcing* heat through the beans. It's possible through either of these methods to get beans that are burned on the outside and still green on the inside, not to mention a room full of smoke.

It is possible, by frequent stirring or shaking, or by use of an electric coffee roaster, to force more heat exposure to each bean, but it still will take some practice. We recommend that you use Colombia beans at first. They seem to come out the best in home roasting.

3.

MAKING GOOD COFFEE STARTS WITH BUYING GOOD COFFEE

Good coffee starts with good beans. The best brewing equipment and methods—important as they are —cannot make up for inferior or stale beans. So looking for the best coffee tastes means looking for the best coffee beans.

To some extent, the search for good coffee involves the search for one or more retail stores whose standards of quality you trust. The Yellow Pages of your phone directory should list the gourmet coffee retailers in your area. They usually fall under such headings as "coffee, retail," "coffee and tea, retail," or even "gourmet foods." In some areas the directory makes no distinction between local mass market coffee

outlets and specialty coffee retailers. If you're not sure
about the type of coffee being sold, call and ask. If you
don't have a coffee store in your area, a search in the
directory of a nearby city may help you find a store
that will mail you coffee for the additional cost of
fourth-class postage. It's important to find one or two
retail outlets knowledgeable about coffee and commit-
ted to quality. Once you feel good about them, you
can usually feel good about their coffee and their rec-
ommendations. Nevertheless, the choices are ulti-
mately yours. To make them wisely, you should be
aware of some basic guidelines for selecting good coffee.

When you buy coffee from the bin, you should be
concerned about four things: 1) the kind of coffee
flavor you want, 2) the degree to which the beans have
been roasted, 3) the freshness of the beans, and 4)
uniformity of bean size and color.

There is no shortcut to deciding what beans or
blends you like. No matter what you read about coffees and their tastes, in order to find out what *you* like
you'll have to experiment by tasting different coffees,
just as you do wines. You'll soon find that each bean,
or blend, in combination with the degree to which it
has been roasted and the time it has been aged, has its
own subtle, distinctive flavor. These flavors will vary
considerably, from deep, full-bodied Sumatra to delicate, light Guatemala; and each can be enjoyed for its
own unique taste.

The second thing to look for in beans is the degree of roast. The degree to which a coffee bean has
been roasted will tell you something about its flavor

and when it will reach a flavor peak from the date of roasting.

It would be nice if there was only one way to properly roast all coffee beans. Unfortunately, this is not the case. Consumers have different taste preferences and coffee roasters have developed their own biases, both in roast equipment and techniques. Therefore, you should taste and compare the different kinds of roasts carried by coffee shops in your area. One shop may sell American coffees the way you like them roasted while another shop's African and Indonesian beans may be roasted more to your liking.

In any roast, light or dark, coffee oils work their way to the surface and evaporate, eventually leaving a dry, rancid, and somewhat rubbery shell. The trick is to grind and brew your coffee soon after roasting, preferably within a week. If the beans have been underroasted, the green juices inside them will produce an undesirable taste. If the beans are overroasted, much of their flavor and aroma will already have been ruined by too much heat. Either way, the beans will not mature properly and will produce inferior coffee.

Just as roasting affects the quality of coffee flavor, it also affects the time that flavor takes to reach a perfect peak. Coffee beans reach flavor peak one to three days after roasting. Usually, flavor in darker roasts will mature more slowly than in lighter roasts. For example, three days after roasting is the best time to begin consuming Celebes Kalossi, an Indonesian bean which is best when roasted darker. Peru and Nicaragua, best roasted light, should be ready for consumption within twenty-four hours.

One more item is worth mentioning before we leave the subject of roasting. Once you have experienced the well-developed taste of coffee at flavor peak, you might find it interesting to backtrack and experience the young, zesty flavor of coffee straight from the roaster. Newly roasted coffee can be a pleasant variation on a familiar taste.

Freshness is the third major factor to consider when buying beans. Remember, coffee, especially roasted coffee, is a perishable fruit. Once beyond its optimum flavor peak, it begins to spoil.

The best way to assure yourself of buying fresh coffee is to know its roasting date. To get this information, ask the coffee merchant. He'll know if he roasts his own, but he may have more difficulty if he buys the beans already roasted. If he is really conscientious, he'll make it his business to know the roasting date of beans he buys elsewhere. He owes it to you and to his business. Beans roasted far away can easily age past their prime in transit if no pains have been taken to store and ship them correctly.

The other reason you should ask the roasting date is because some shops will leave their coffee out until it sells, regardless of its age. Be especially wary of this possibility in retail stores that carry whole bean coffee only as a sideline. Beans begin to stale noticeably a week after roasting if left in a display bin or burlap bag.

If you don't know the coffee's roasting date, you'll have to rely on your own senses to determine bean freshness.

First, look at the beans. Overaged beans have a

tendency to be dry. Dark roasted beans may be covered by a watery film that produces a splotchy, mottled appearance. A fresh bean is reaching flavor peak when the oils within begin to collect on the surface and evaporate. These oils will often give the beans a shiny, grease-stained appearance. This visual test is pretty reliable for darker roasts, but on light roasts surface oils aren't as prominent.

So, take another step. Bite a bean. A fresh bean has a brittle, delicate texture and gives off a bright burst of flavor. Old beans are hard, somewhat rubbery, and dry. They crack more than they crumble, and they are flat compared to the taste of a fresh bean.

Once you've bitten the bean in half, munch one half and look at the other. A good light or medium roast, when broken open, should reveal a bright, straw-colored chaff in the center of the bean. If it does, you have what is called a "brilliant" roast. If the chaff is white, the bean probably has been under-roasted. In this case, the natural flavor of the bean will not have been developed and, therefore, will not produce a good cup of coffee. In good darker roasted coffees, the chaff will tend to be dark also, but not as dark as the bean itself.

Uniformity of bean size, shape, and color, the fourth factor to consider in buying beans, is important because it will tell you something about the original quality of a batch of beans. Even high-quality Arabicas are sometimes "filled" with lower-quality beans of the same crop; or the exporting country doesn't send its premium crop to gourmet coffee buyers in North America. A batch of mixed- or lower-quality roast beans isn't difficult to detect. Bean size will vary as much as 40 percent. Some beans will be oddly shaped. And bean color will range from dark brown to mustard yellow. Usually it is the same beans that are small, misshaped, and off-color.

Peeking in the Back Room

Most consumers must judge the quality of coffee beans after they are roasted. But if you patronize a coffee store which roasts its own, you have an opportunity to examine and evaluate green beans as well.

Remember, roasting for the most part will not improve the quality of the beans. It can only bring out to best advantage the flavor lying dormant within the bean. So if you see a batch of low-quality beans waiting for the roaster, you should be wary of roasted beans sold by the store.

In green beans you should be concerned about uniformity of size, shape, and color, just as in roasted beans. The best quality, higher-grown Arabicas have a consistency of shape and size and are usually blue or gray-green in color. Pronounced differences in size, shape, and color mean that the beans have been purchased by the merchant without regard to differences in maturity and quality. Various colorations other than blue or gray-green suggest certain deficiencies in bean quality. Yellow beans for instance, indicate that the coffee was picked while still immature or that it's an old crop. Red beans were probably overripe when picked or were improperly washed.

Mottled beans suggest uneven drying procedures. Black beans result from plant disease.

Although good coffee is now readily available through coffee specialty stores, you should not assume that all of these stores are equally conscientious about the quality of their product. For the sake of your taste buds and your pocketbook it would be a good idea to try several different coffee stores (if several are available) and compare beans, roast quality, freshness, and price. No matter what the coffee merchants say about their product, trust your taste. Differences in quality and freshness are apparent in properly brewed coffee.

Storing Coffee

Because coffee is perishable it should be treated with the care you must give any perishable food. With the passage of time, ground or whole bean coffee stales from the influence of oxygen, moisture, and heat. Of course, ground coffee, because it exposes more surface area to these influences, stales much faster. A grind can stale in hours or days. It takes one to three weeks for coffee beans to show signs of staleness. One of these signs is a sweet, cocoalike odor. In the cup, the coffee will taste bland and rancid, and the aroma will be flat.

The best way to prevent deterioration of your coffee is to buy it in small quantities so that it won't be around more than a week. Since beans stay fresh longer than ground coffee, you would be better off to buy beans and grind them at home as you make each pot. After some experience, you should have a pretty good notion of how much coffee will last you for a week. To start with, however, figure that a pound of coffee will yield fifty to sixty cups. Using that as a guide, compute your consumption rate and buy your coffee accordingly.

When you purchase your coffee from a whole bean store it will probably be put in a glassine-lined or plastic bag. When you get home, transfer it to an airtight container and place it in the refrigerator if it has reached its peak or is past its peak. Refrigeration dramatically reduces flavor loss. However, if the newly roasted coffee has not yet reached its peak, transfer it to the sealed container and leave it on the shelf at room temperature until it has. Coffee refrigerated too soon after roasting may never reach its flavor peak. You would want to refrigerate a brand new roast only if you like a "green" taste. An old-fashioned storage jar with a wire clamp lid is perfect for keeping coffee. However, any jar that seals tightly will do.

Buying beans in small weekly quantities may be impractical if you live too far away or if you buy by mail. In that case, the best course may be to buy beans in large quantities and freeze them in an airtight moisture-proof container. Freezing will alter coffee flavor slightly, just as it will any fruit or vegetable. But the slight flavor change caused by freezing good quality coffee is preferable to letting it stale, and far preferable to buying anything put out by mass market coffee processors.

If you like coffee with a mature taste and some depth to it, you should let your beans thaw for about

ten minutes after you remove them from the freezer. Grinding frozen beans and brewing the grind immediately tends to give the coffee a young, immature taste. Again, think of coffee as a fruit. As with any frozen fruit, for its flavor to be released, you have to give it time to thaw. If you do buy your coffee in quantity and freeze it, you should thaw it (about a week's supply at a time) in the refrigerator. This gradual, limited warming will cut down on condensation in the container. The less condensation there is, the less moisture will be absorbed into the coffee.

Growing Your Own Coffee

We wouldn't seriously suggest that you grow your own coffee as an alternative to buying coffee. But coffee plants add a nice touch to a room—and who knows, with patience and luck, they might give you a bit of the freshest coffee in town.

Coffee is a very sensitive plant. A coffee merchant we know swears that the coffee plants in his store thrive when business is good and do poorly when it isn't. A coffee plant requires acid soil, humidity, warm temperatures (normal room temperature is fine), sunlight part of the day, and indirect light the rest of the time. The plant should be watered thoroughly every seven to fourteen days, or when it's just beginning to droop. We've heard you can give your plant a little extra boost by feeding it some lukewarm coffee beverage. Sugar or cream won't be necessary.

You may be able to germinate plants from green beans acquired at the coffee store, but you're probably better off to start with seedlings from a plant store. By the time green coffee beans arrive at the retail roaster, they will more than likely be dead as seeds.

Once your coffee sprouts are going well, settle back. It takes five years for a coffee plant to bear fruit (if you're lucky). If you *are* lucky, your plant will let you know it by producing snowy white blossoms similar in appearance and fragrance to jasmine. You should help the plant pollinate itself by brushing across the flowers with a small, soft paintbrush.

When coffee cherries begin to appear, they will be green. When they become ruby red or purple, they are ready to be picked. They should be processed along the lines discussed in Chapter 8, "Coffee from Bush to Bag." Incidentally, don't expect more than a couple handfuls of roastable green beans.

4.
GRINDING
AND
GRINDERS

Grinding is the first step in transforming roast coffee beans into coffee beverage. Grinding breaks each bean into a larger surface area, exposing its delicate flavors and aromas so they can be extracted by water in the brewing process.

If you are just getting into good coffee, you may want to have it ground initially by the coffee store before you commit yourself to the expense of a grinder. Coffee merchants grind beans for their customers at no extra charge. This will give you time to decide what your grinding needs are and to check out some of the grinding equipment available in your locale. If you do buy ground coffee, be mindful that it stales much faster than whole bean coffee. Keep it refrigerated in a sealed container and use it within a reasonable time—at least within a week.

Whether you have your beans ground at the shop or grind them yourself, it is important that the degree of the grind fit the brewing system you use. Many manufacturers of brewing equipment recommend the grind to use, but a few of them are incorrect. If you're not sure, ask the coffee retailer. Coffee store people are usually familiar with most of the current brewing systems and their grind requirements.

Sooner or later, as you form definite preferences for the coffee you drink and the way you brew it, you will probably want to buy your own grinder. It not only will allow you to keep your coffee fresher by buying it in whole bean form, it also will treat you to one of the nicer parts of enjoying good coffee: the pungent aroma and crunching rattle of whole beans going through the coffee mill. It's a preview to the good smell of brewing coffee or the first taste of a freshly made cup. In addition, a coffee grinder often adds a decorative touch to a kitchen.

Determining a grind to fit your brewing system isn't a complex task, mainly because there are only three kinds of grinds used in 95 percent of all coffee brewing: perk or regular grind (akin to sawdust in texture), drip grind (medium fine texture), and fine grind (verging on powdery). Two so-called border grinds apply to the other 5 percent. They are coarse or open-pot grind for boiling "cowboy" coffee, and powder grind used mainly for boiling Turkish coffee. Although there are some variations in the degree of each of the three main grinds, you will have no trouble arriving at the right grind for your system with a bit of experimentation. The main thing to avoid is using one grind for a system which requires another kind of grind. For example, a perk grind used in a drip filter will result in underextraction, and a weak cup of coffee. A drip grind in a percolator (which we don't favor anyway) will result in overextracted, bitter coffee.

GRINDING SYSTEMS

Home coffee grinding equipment generally falls into two categories, electric mills and hand-operated mills. Some electric mills and all hand mills pulverize coffee beans by crushing them between the surfaces of two metal burrs, one stationary and one moving. Hence, they are often called burr mills. Other electric mills use a moving blade, like a propeller, to chop the beans into grounds. Some people use kitchen blenders to grind coffee but blenders—except for one brand which has a coffee grinding attachment—have a couple of drawbacks. Because they haven't been designed to grind coffee, blenders usually produce an inconsistent grind, coarse at the top of the batch and powdery at the bottom. An inconsistent grind like this is undesirable because part of it doesn't fit your brewing system, no matter what kind it is. Blenders are also inconvenient because they have to be cleaned every time you switch from coffee grinding to blending or vice versa.

Your choice of a coffee mill will depend on your own preferences, but some of the main things you will probably consider in buying a coffee mill are looks, cost, grinding efficiency, and durability. Things you should add to that checklist include bean capacity, capability to adjust degrees of grind, ease of cleaning, and the kind of noise the machine makes grinding beans. Before you make your choice, you might like to know something about these characteristics as they apply to each kind of mill.

Hand Mills

Hand mills are usually more ornamental than electric mills and are available in a wide range of prices and quality. Some cost as little as ten dollars while a functional antique mill can soar as high as $1,000. The better hand mills, even the fine European ones, are reasonably priced (twenty to fifty dollars) and do as good a job as quality electric mills.

There are two basic kinds of hand mills, the box or lap grinder, and the wall or shelf-mounted grinder. The typical box grinder is either square or rectangular, five to eight inches in diameter, and wooden. The bean receptacle and grinding crank sit atop the mechanism and the operator has to turn the crank in a clockwise motion parallel to the floor. This is done most easily in a sitting position while the grinder is held in the lap or gripped between the legs—hence the name lap grinder. This grinder is attractive, often in an Early American motif, and easy to store because of its size and compact shape. Its principal drawback is its small grinding surface. Larger grinding surfaces pulverize beans more efficiently and uniformly, and generally last longer. The small grinding surface of the typical box grinder restricts bean capacity, requires several minutes of grinding, and wears the grinding surfaces more quickly. Box grinders also have a tendency to spit a few beans out of the receptacle during

grinding. Because cheap, inferior box grinders are sometimes purchased by gift and department stores, you may feel more comfortable shopping for a box grinder at a coffee store or kitchen implement store adept at judging the quality of such a specialized item. A Turkish coffee grinder, typically a cylindrical metal mill that can be gripped in the hand, is constructed along the same lines as a box grinder but has finer burrs to produce the powder grind required in Turkish coffee.

One of the most popular mounted grinders operates much like an old-fashioned cast-iron meat grinder and has the same appearance. The mounted cast-iron grinder is distinguished from the box grinder primarily by the location of the crank on the side of the mechanism and the fact that it is usually mounted by clamps or screws to a counter edge or wall. Beans are fed into a receptacle at the top, pulverized by a cone-shaped burr, and deposited in a tray or pan. Although this grinder comes in a variety of sizes from about seventeen to forty dollars, it is usually larger and more efficient than the box grinder. Compared with the box grinder, it features a larger grinding surface, a crank easier to turn because of its length and its vertical motion around a stable axis, a shorter grinding time, and a more consistent grind.

A wall-mounted mill with side crank, enclosed china hopper, wood backboard, and conventional box-type grinding burr is also available. This mill is not only attractive but offers the added advantage of temporary bean storage. A rubber gasket between the hopper and the grinding mechanism creates a good enough seal to hold bean freshness a few days. If

you go through coffee at a fairly rapid rate and want to avoid going to the shelf or refrigerator each time you need to grind beans, this mill will save you some labor.

In both box mills and mounted mills there are three other characteristics to consider: adjustment for degree of grind, type of metal in the burr mechanism, and ease of cleaning.

Every burr mill has some kind of adjustment for tightening and loosening the fit of the two metal grinding surfaces to a finer or coarser grind. But a friend of ours who takes his coffee seriously recommends that you buy a grinder with an adjustment that's somewhat hidden from plain sight. His reasoning is that if the adjustment is too conspicuous, either a child or guest may find it and play with it, moving your setting from where you have worked so hard to get it. "You can be in a bad mood for a week if that happens," he cautions.

The burr mechanism on hand mills is usually made of cast iron or hardened, die-cut steel, although some manufacturers are marketing a mill with nickel- or chrome-plated grinding surfaces. The steel grinder, more prevalent among European models, usually costs more, but it has a life of thirty to fifty years. Grinders with the softer cast-iron mechanism usually last ten to twenty years. Plated grinding mechanisms may last a bit longer than cast iron, but eventually the plating will wear or flake off the base metal. Incidentally, when you first buy a burr mill, you should break it in. To do this, tighten the burr adjustment firmly, run a small amount of coffee beans through it, and throw away the grind. This will clean the grinding surfaces of any residual metal filings and packing oil, and will give the metal a light, protective coat of oil from the ground beans.

In your coffee mill, as in your brewing equipment, ease of cleaning is an important factor to consider. Most burr grinders are relatively self-cleaning because a new batch of beans pushes through most residue from the last grinding. But some coffee oils and powder will collect in out-of-the-way crevices in the mechanism and become rancid over a period of time. Therefore, a hand mill should be easy to disassemble for cleaning. To clean the grinding surfaces, every few months rinse them in hot water (don't use soap) and dry them with a towel, or simply brush them clean with a stiff brush (but not one with a metal bristle). If you favor dark roast coffee, a simpler though less thorough method of cleaning is occasionally to run a small quantity of light roast beans through the mill. Dark roasts leave behind more oils and powdery residue than light roasts. Light roast beans will absorb some of them.

One last word on hand mills. If you prefer to buy an antique mill, make sure that it is functional. Many of the antiques on the market will probably be impractical for everyday use. Many of them can't be adjusted for finer grinds, and the burr mechanism in very old mills may be worn beyond usefulness.

Electric Mills

Electric coffee mills seem to have a lot of appeal, particularly the blade grinders. Their central attraction, of course, is convenience. It's easier to hold down a

button for twenty or so seconds than to turn a crank. Some coffee purists claim that both blade and burr electric mills (compared to hand mills) generate too much heat from friction during the grinding process, thereby downgrading the coffee's taste. If they do, we believe it's too minor to detect. But as a point of information, you may be interested to know that electric blade grinders, because they repeatedly chop the same grind, generate slightly more heat and friction.

The grinding mechanism in electric burr mills is similar to that of hand mills, but burr mills have some distinctive characteristics beyond their use of electric power. Generally, they are costlier, slower, and noiser than comparable-quality hand mills. However, they are generally reliable, produce a consistent grind, and are easy to use. They invariably contain a die-cut steel grinding mechanism.

A few things to look for in a good electric burr mill include ease of cleaning, hopper size, and quality of the coupling between the grinder and the bin where the coffee is deposited. The spout where the grinds are spit out and the receiving bin should interlock solidly. Some models have a foam rubber pad coupling between the grinder and the receptacle. When the mill gets older, the foam rubber padding may break down, allowing coffee to shoot out the sides.

If you want to grind your coffee with minimum effort and time, we recommend an electric blade grinder. Most blade grinders consist of a motor-driven, stainless steel chopping blade which sits at the bottom of a small hopper under a clear plastic cover.

The time the blade is run determines the degree of the grind, so a blade grinder is somewhat trickier to control for degree of grind than a burr mill. With some practice, however, you can become fairly adept at grinding your coffee the way you want it. For example, a friend of ours finds that in just twenty seconds his particular blade grinder produces a fairly good grind for drip filter brewing. Although they produce a less consistent grind, blade mills have a number of advantages over electric burr mills. They generally cost less, grind coffee faster, clean easily with the wipe of a dry paper towel, and store conveniently because of their compact size. In a blade grinder, as well as an electric burr grinder, the machine should have a safety feature which automatically prevents it from operating unless the chopping or milling mechanism is covered and inaccessible to your fingers.

Whether you favor an electric or a hand grinder, there are a few precautions you should definitely take before you make a purchase. First, compare prices. It isn't uncommon to see as much as a five-dollar difference in the price of the same grinder sold in different stores. Second, make sure the machine you purchase has a warranty. You're even better off if the manufacturer has repair and service arrangements with a nearby appliance repair business. Third, try out the grinder you favor on some whole beans. Most coffee shops, and even some kitchen appliance stores, have floor models and a supply of beans available for demonstration.

5.

BREWING
METHODS
AND
EQUIPMENT

PRINCIPLES OF BREWING GOOD COFFEE

Brewing is the passing of hot water through coffee grounds long enough for it to extract the soluble oils, waxes, and gases that give the coffee beverage its pleasant flavor and aroma. It sounds simple, but most people have been doing it wrong for years. Brewing a good pot of coffee requires no more time or energy than brewing a mediocre pot. It simply requires that you follow a few basic guidelines.

We concur with six guidelines identified by the Coffee Brewing Center of the Pan-American Coffee Bureau. They are:

1. Begin with clean equipment.

2. Use the best water available.

3. Brew your coffee at the proper temperature.

4. Use the correct grind for your brewing system.

5. Use the correct proportion of water to coffee.

6. Brew your coffee the proper length of time.

Following is our own elaboration on these steps.

1. Begin with clean equipment. The German statesman Bismarck is said to have remarked, "The recipe for good coffee is simple—use a new pot every time." Even in its day this advice was erroneous for pots with linings like tin that needed breaking in to seal microscopic pores and eliminate the raw taste of new metal. And today that advice would be just as misleading for pots made of aluminum or tin-lined copper and brass. But the Chancellor's sentiment is useful. If brewing equipment is not washed or at least rinsed after every use, it will collect a visible oil film that can add a bitter taste to the coffee. Even brewers made of glass, porcelain, or stainless steel—which don't need breaking in—will collect these oils.

However, it's important to remember that cleaning coffee equipment requires a bit more discretion than cleaning other kitchen items. For one thing, you should not use soap because it can leave a film (despite rinsing) that will flavor your coffee. To clean coffee equipment, you should brush or wipe it out, using hot water, and then rinse it with hot water. If you don't feel comfortable using just water, try a baking soda solution and rinse thoroughly. Baking soda neutralizes existing flavors and leaves no trace of its own. If oils tend to build up despite your regular cleaning, you might try a commercially available pot destainer. Generally, we don't prefer this treatment for metal brewers (excepting stainless steel) because the destainers contain very strong chemicals that literally scour out even the coffee oils sealing raw metal pores, requiring you to break in your coffee maker again.

Perhaps the strongest caution we can issue on cleaning is that you never scrub your coffee maker with anything abrasive. This kind of treatment will leaves scratches and pits in soft metal and damage the polished surface of stainless steel. Soft metal pots will require breaking in again, but that will be the least of your troubles. The crevices left by abrasives may be too small for you to see, but they will trap pockets of coffee oils hard to clean out and large enough to taint your coffee when they become rancid.

Some brewing equipment contains inner surfaces that are difficult to get at. For the most part, the use of special brushes and frequent washing will prevent coffee oil buildup on these surfaces but won't be able to remove mineral deposits left from the brewing water. Even if you live in an area which doesn't have hard water, mineral deposits can still build up in your coffee maker over a period of time, especially on metal surfaces. The best way to deal with this problem is occasionally to run a brewing cycle using one part white distilled vinegar and three to five parts water. Then follow it up with two cycles using only water in order to flush out any vinegar residue. This method, which is also used to clean steam irons, works very effectively.

2. Use the best water available. Coffee is 98

percent water, so the quality of the water you use is quite important. One of our coffee purist acquaintances insists that distilled water should be used in brewing coffee, but we can't go that far. Generally, if the water you normally drink is acceptable as is, then it will be acceptable for making coffee. On the other hand, whatever taste is apparent in the water will also be apparent in your coffee. Brewing your coffee stronger won't mask a bad water taste.

Naturally soft or slightly hard water is the best water to use. Moderately hard water is satisfactory if no unpleasant tastes or odors are present. However, hard water hastens the buildup of mineral deposits in your equipment. Artificially softened water is about the worst thing you can use to brew coffee. The chemicals in the softeners form a gelatinous mass in the coffee grounds. This slows the passage of water through the grounds, giving it time to absorb the bitter flavors of the grounds along with the good ones.

If you don't have naturally soft water in your area and you dislike coffee with a hard water taste, then you should consider using bottled spring water. You may find the good taste worth the extra expense. If the water in your area has chemical odors, too much chlorine or other taste impurities in it, you might want to install an activated carbon filter on your water tap. This will remove most bad odors and tastes except for large amounts of sulfur.

One other word of caution. If you're using tap water to brew coffee, begin with cold water. The thermostatic controls of some automatic brewing systems require this anyway. But the main reason to avoid hot water is that it acquires a flat taste from lying so long in the hot water tank.

3. Brew your coffee at the proper temperature. Water temperature is an important factor in flavor extraction. The best brewing temperature is 195° to 205° F., just shy of the 212° boiling point. Unless you have had personal experience with a particular piece of automatic brewing equipment, you have only the manufacturer's claims to assure you that the mechanism is brewing coffee at the correct temperature. But if you use a manual brewing system, say a drip filter brewer or a plunge pot, you can control the temperature easily. By taking a few seconds to bring a kettle of rapidly boiling water from the heating element to the grounds in the filter cone or brewing chamber, you will lower the temperature of the water from 212° to the proper temperature. If you don't bring the hot water to the system this soon, it will cool below the optimum brewing temperature. Even water at 190° will give your coffee a slightly washed-out taste because it isn't hot enough to extract flavor efficiently. If you do brew coffee in a drip filter, pour only enough water in the cone to fill it halfway, and then return the kettle to the heating element to continue boiling. When you're ready to continue pouring, your water will be at the right temperature.

4. Use the correct grind for your brewing system. As noted in the previous chapter, it's important to match the grind of your beans to your brewing system. The finer the grind you use, the greater the flavor extraction, so you have to gauge the grind to the *length of time* and to the *way* water passes through the grounds in your brewer. Because a percolator recirculates water through the grounds a number of times, it will always require a sawdustlike perk or regular grind. Drip pots, in which the water passes through the grounds only once, require a finer textured drip grind. Some filter drip pots, depending on the paper, will work well with a near-powdery fine grind. As we've noted, many manufacturers of brewing equipment recommend the grind to use, but it's a good idea to check this information with your coffee merchant. Better yet, experiment yourself. There's no substitute for your own experience.

5. Use the correct proportion of water to coffee. As a general rule, two level tablespoons of grind per six-ounce measure of water is a good extraction ratio. Another way to look at this proportion is one part coffee to six parts water. When you first buy a brewing system, check the calibration markings in the grounds container and beverage container to determine whether or not they are reliable. What is meant by a ground coffee measure or a cup varies with manufacturers. In addition, what you consider a cup may vary with the manufacturer's notion of a cup. For example, one of the most popular manual drip systems on the market will hold only three and a half 6-ounce cups at the mark which indicates four cups. The amount of coffee at that level fills four average teacups but only two and a half small mugs.

Although the one-to-six ratio seems to be favored by a lot of coffee drinkers, you should regard it only as a point of departure. Your own preference in coffee strength should be the main consideration. If you like stronger coffee, begin with more grounds. But *never* pour freshly brewed coffee back through the spent grounds. This will extract some of the less desirable flavors left behind in the first dripping and won't pick up any additional strength among the good flavors. There are two ways to make milder coffee. One is to begin with less grounds. The other is to add hot water to the beverage after it has been brewed. We favor the first method for making just a few cups. However, the other method is useful if you are making coffee for a lot of people. In fact, you can save yourself the trouble of brewing two batches of coffee by brewing one batch at double strength and matching the freshly brewed beverage with an equal amount of hot water.

6. *Brew your coffee the proper length of time.* This is a very important step in coffee brewing and one you should keep in mind if you are about to buy an automatic brewing system. The majority of automatic brewing systems on the market fall short in this one respect.

The brewing process begins at the moment hot water touches the ground coffee and stops when the last of the water has gone through. The correct brewing time is wholly dependent on the texture of the grind. For a fine grind, the brewing time should be four minutes or less; for a drip grind, four to six minutes; for regular or perk grind, six to eight minutes. Water in contact with coffee grounds beyond these time limits will extract the worst flavors.

Keeping Freshly Brewed Coffee

After coffee is brewed, it begins to deteriorate. It gradually loses its aromatic qualities and it begins to break down chemically. This process isn't noticeable until after about fifteen to thirty minutes. After thirty minutes, the beverage gets progressively darker, loses its aroma, and begins to take on a strong to bitter taste, especially if it is left on a heating element. In restaurants which pay attention to their coffee, you may have seen a waitress hold a pot of coffee up to the light to check its color. If the reddish tint was gone, the coffee probably was thrown out.

Coffee tastes best as soon as it's brewed, but there are some things you can do to keep a batch of coffee from going bad before it can be consumed. Holding the fresh coffee at a temperature between 180 and 190° is the best way to slow its deterioration. Some automatic brewing systems have a built-in heating element for this purpose and some manufacturers of manual drip filter systems market small electric heating elements which supposedly keep a carafe of coffee at the right temperature. However, we favor holding fresh coffee in a glass-lined, vacuum-insulated serving container akin to a thermos bottle. Coffee on a heating element continues to "cook" from the steady input of heat in the element, and it isn't much good after fifteen minutes. A vacuum container is better because it evenly turns back heat originating from the liquid itself. Coffee held in such a container can taste reasonably good thirty minutes to an hour after brewing. One manufacturer now makes a drip filter brewing system which employs a vacuum container as the carafe that directly receives the dripped coffee. If you use such a drip system, it isn't necessary to preheat the container.

We'd like to add a word of caution if you are thinking of buying a ceramic drip system, serving pot, or set of serving mugs. As beautiful as these potter's crafts are, they are less than ideal for making coffee or holding it at the proper temperature because they dissipate heat. If you do brew coffee or serve it with ceramic ware, be sure to preheat the pottery with very hot tapwater before filling it with coffee.

BREWING METHODS AND SYSTEMS

The coffee brewing system you decide to use should be one which produces excellent coffee while meeting your particular coffee-making needs. Things you might want to consider are brewing volume, ease of operation, ease of cleaning, durability, and warranty protection. Since most manufacturers recommend that you don't use less than three-quarters of a brewer's capacity, you may even want to have two different brewing systems—a small one for your personal coffee drinking and a larger one for entertaining.

The two most popular methods of brewing coffee in the United States today are percolation and drip filter brewing. Until recently, percolation was the more common brewing system, primarily because of its long traditional use. However, drip brewers appear to be taking over the market as more people discover that drip brewing produces a better cup of coffee and involves less cleanup. However, there are other ways of making coffee, each suited to different tastes and circumstances. These include less common drip

methods, plunge-pot brewing, plain boiling, and cold water extraction. In the following pages we'll discuss the way all these coffee making systems work, along with some of their strengths and disadvantages.

Percolation

Combined with the aroma of fresh brewing coffee, the rhythmic sound of water surging through a stove-top or electric percolator is a pleasant experience. But that's the best thing that can be said for perk brewing. There are better ways to make coffee.

Percolation violates several rules of brewing good coffee. The most important of these is that it overextracts coffee grounds by steadily recirculating extracted coffee beverage through those grounds. Water heated at the bottom of the pot rises through a central tube, sprays over a perforated basket filled with ground coffee, and then drips back into the bottom of the pot. Each pleasant sounding surge of water in the pot means that the grounds are being overextracted and will yield their bitterness along with their good flavor. The heavy coffee aroma that perking puts into a room is evidence that the aroma isn't being infused into the coffee beverage where it belongs. Another rule violated by most electric percolators is that they take more than the maximum eight minutes recommended in a perk brewing cycle. This produces more overextraction. In addition, percolators boil first their water supply and then the extracted coffee beverage as they perk. This defies the rule that coffee beverage should not be extracted or heated above 205°. Many percolators also produce a cup of coffee containing sediment from the grounds.

Incidentally, the coffee extract that is dried or freeze-dried to make mass market instant coffee is perked and reperked in huge percolators until it is supersaturated with the best and worst of coffee flavors. This kind of coffee, known as soluble coffee in the trade, is not only made badly but is usually made from poor or mediocre beans.

Drip Brewing

Drip brewing is a very old coffee-making method which has acquired recent popularity through the addition of filter paper to the process. Percolators are generally cheaper than drip equipment, but the booming market for drip brewers indicates a growing public awareness about what makes a good pot of coffee.

Drip brewing is simply the dripping of hot water once through ground coffee. If you begin with good beans and follow the six guidelines we've discussed, your payoff will be delicious coffee.

If you decide to buy a drip brewer, you have the option of either a manual or an automatic system. The manual system usually consists of an open-top funnel cone with a small bottom opening that is inserted into the narrow top of a carafe so that the whole affair has the configuration of a bow tie stood on end. A cone-shaped filter paper is usually inserted into the cone and ground coffee is measured onto the paper. Then hot water is poured over the grounds to extract coffee flavor and pass through the filter as clarified coffee into the carafe below.

Manual drip filter systems have several attractive characteristics. First, they are cheaper than automatic systems (some of which exceed fifty dollars). In fact, one very popular manual drip system that makes an excellent pot of coffee sells for about six dollars; and the filter papers for it cost about three or four cents each. Second, manual drip brewers allow you complete control to adhere to proper brewing guidelines. By contrast, automatic brewers control water temperature and brewing time internally. For these brewing variables to be correct in an automatic system, the manufacturer has to have programmed the machine correctly (a number of them haven't). If you inadvertently run out of filter papers, the manual drip system has the advantage of enabling you to substitute a paper towel in the cone for the filter. Automatic drip systems usually require odd or basket-shaped filter papers that make paper towel substitution difficult. Some coffee people gag at the suggestion of using a paper towel for a filter, and we don't recommend it on a regular basis. But it does work in a pinch if you use plain white single-layer paper. Hard-core coffee purists don't sanction even drip filters because they impart a filter taste to the coffee that can be detected by the sensitive tongue. We don't think it makes enough difference to worry about.

What some people regard as a disadvantage to the manual drip brewer is the fussing around it takes.

After the ground coffee is measured into the paper cone, water has to be boiled separately. Then an initial measure of hot water (a quarter to half a cone) has to be poured over the grounds. Then that has to be allowed to pass through. Then another dose or two of hot water has to be added in half-cone measures (amid care that wet grounds are washed off the sides of the filter cone so all the coffee grounds are used). The involvement of this process can be a ritual joy, but it also can be a pain if you are trying to visit with guests or attend to other chores at the same time.

The automatic drip brewer is a lot more convenient. All you have to do is put ground coffee in a filter basket, pour cold water in a special compartment, and make sure the carafe is in place. The machine does the rest. Many of them have an automatic heating element but, as we've mentioned, we favor holding freshly brewed coffee in a vacuum-insulated serving container.

The most important thing you have to find out in shopping for an automatic drip brewer is whether it conforms to the standards of good brewing, especially the proper water temperature and length of brewing time. Ideally, you should test the system yourself, but that usually isn't possible unless you know someone who owns a drip system like the one you are considering. Coffee store retailers usually don't have brewing systems set up for demonstration, although they should. Usually, however, the merchant will be able to supply some particulars on the quality and workings of various brewers. In addition, the manufacturer's brochure may be helpful if it is specific enough. The drawback to most such brochures is that they merely say they conform to recommended brewing standards without saying whose standards or without demonstrating a knowledge of what those standards are.

Perhaps the safest path to follow in shopping for an automatic drip brewer is to look for the Coffee Brewing Center seal of approval. Any brewer bearing this seal will have passed up to 110 tests of its conformity to proper brewing standards. As of this writing, eighteen brewing systems on the market have this seal of approval.

French Drip Pot, Neopolitan Pot, Vacuum Pot

French drip, Neopolitan, and vacuum pots are all variations of the drip system. They are old methods but quite good if you enjoy thick coffee.

The classic French drip pot is made of porcelain but has an American counterpart of similar metal design. The drip pot consists of a serving pitcher atop which is fitted a smaller drip basket cylinder with a perforated bottom. Ground coffee is measured into the basket and hot water is poured in from the top. The holes in the porcelain drip pot usually take a coarser grind. The French-style drip pot is an elegant piece of serving ware. The porcelain pot is often considered more attractive than metal but it's quite a bit more expensive (fifteen to thirty dollars for porcelain, five to twenty dollars for metal). Like any ceramic used in coffee brewing or serving, the porcelain pot

should be heated with a temporary filling of hot tap water before it is drip filled, otherwise the ceramic will draw off much of the heat in the fresh coffee. Of course, an obvious drawback to the porcelain pot is its fragility. Metal drip pots can survive a dropping now and then.

A little device called a mono filter is available for dripping a single cup of coffee. It is a metal drip basket which fits over the rim of a coffee cup. Ground coffee is measured into the perforated metal bottom of the basket and then a second perforated metal disc is placed over the grounds to spread hot water poured into the basket. This drip device produces a good cup of coffee but requires as much attention as a manual drip filter brewing system.

A Neopolitan pot is a drip brewer which saves you the trouble of boiling water separately and manually pouring it through coffee grounds. This pot actually consists of two metal pots, a water pot and a serving pot, which fit together snugly at their tops. When the two are joined together, whichever pot is on top is upside down. Water is boiled in the water pot and then the whole assembly is taken off the heat and turned over so the water can drip down through an enclosed basket of coffee into the serving pot. In the preparation of Neopolitan coffee, water is measured into the water pot below a small pinhole near the upper rim. A smaller metal cylinder with a closed, perforated basket containing ground coffee is inserted open end down into the water pot so the dry coffee sits above the water level. A small groove in the coffee basket must be lined up with the steam pinhole. Then

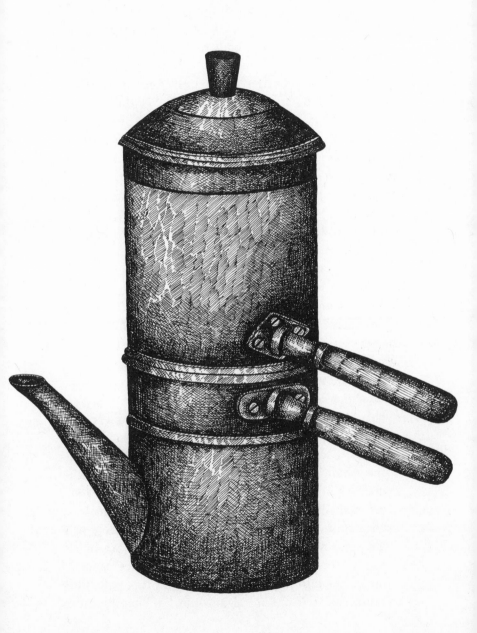

the serving pitcher half of the pot is inserted upside down over the opening of the water pot so the handle of each pot is aligned with the handle of the other. With the water pot on the bottom, the brewer is placed over a burner at medium heat until steam rushes out the pinhole, indicating that the water is boiling. Then the pot is removed from the heat and turned over. Water drips down through the perforated basket containing the ground coffee and into the serving pot. After four or five minutes have passed, the water pot and drip basket are removed and a lid is placed on the serving pot. Then the coffee is ready to be poured. Like the porcelain or metal drip pot, the Neopolitan pot has a handsome, antique look. Depending on metal and hand crafting, a Neopolitan pot sells for four to twenty-four dollars.

Vacuum pots are not used much for coffee making any more, although some stores still carry them. They make good coffee but they seem to have lost a following because of their susceptibility to breakage and the advent of more convenient brewing systems. The vacuum pot consists of two clear, somewhat squat glass chambers: the one on the bottom is a simple carafe with a handle, and the one above is an open-top container with a glass tube at the bottom extending into the carafe below. The top bowl fits snugly into the opening of the carafe chamber by a rubber gasket collar. A small pull spring connected to the bottom of the glass tube holds a cloth or metal filter assembly or a glass strainer in place at the bottom of the top bowl.

In the preparation of vacuum-pot coffee, water is measured into the carafe and brought to a boil. Fine grind coffee is measured into the top chamber after the filter has been secured in place and the carafe is removed from the heat so the two chambers can be fitted together. The pot is returned to the heating element on reduced heat. Water rises through the tube and filter and is allowed to infuse with the ground coffee in the chamber above for about a minute. The pot is removed from the heat and the coffee liquid passes back through the filter and down the tube into the carafe within two minutes, partially because of gravity, partially because of the vacuum in the carafe chamber created by its cooling. The upper bowl is removed before serving.

Plunge Pot

The plunge pot is the true gourmet's brewer. It produces an excellent thick coffee that is suitable for any occasion and is ideal after dinner. It consists of two parts, a cylindrical glass beaker with a handle on the outside, and a flat, stainless steel filter screen fitted precisely to the walls of the beaker like a piston. The screen is connected at its center to a long plunge rod which also passes through a small center hole in the lid of the pot. In the brewing of plunge-pot coffee, the plunger assembly is removed and ground coffee is measured into the pot. We recommend drip grind for European-made pots and regular or perk grind for American models. However, you'll arrive at your own grind preference with some experimentation. After the coffee is in the pot, hot water is added and stirred once or twice to set up a swirling motion that increases the infusion of coffee flavor in the water. After three

and a half to five and a half minutes, the lid is placed on the pot and the filter is firmly pushed to the bottom of the pot by means of the plunger rod. Once the grounds are pressed to the bottom of the beaker, the coffee should be served immediately. We recommend that you try this brewing system with Sumatra or Celebes, either alone or blended with Kona. *That's* coffee drinking.

Open Pot

Open-pot brewing is the method that yields the legendary cowboy or hobo coffee. If you're camping on the road, or find yourself in some other situation where a special coffee-brewing sysem isn't available, you should be versed in open-pot brewing. In this method, water is measured into a clean pot and brought to a boil. Immediately after the pot is removed from heat, two tablespoons of coarse ground coffee per six ounces of water are added. The coffee is steeped for six to ten minutes and then a quarter to half a cup of cold water is added to help settle the grounds. The coffee is then poured carefully in order not to stir up the settled grounds.

Cold Water Extract

If you occasionally like a cup of coffee without the labor of brewing, cold water extraction is your best alternative to instant coffee. In this system, coffee is literally soaked in cold water, producing a highly concentrated coffee extract that can be stored in a refrigerator and added to boiling water to make an instant cup of coffee. It can also be used in iced coffee or cooking. Sometimes called coffee nectar or coffee essence, cold water extract makes a very smooth but bland cup of coffee. This coffee-making method simply doesn't capture many of the flavors and the aroma that hot water extraction does. However, it is very convenient, and some doctors recommend it for people who suffer acid stomach trouble from brewed coffee.

The cold water extractor, which ranges in price from about fifteen to forty-five dollars and comes in several different sizes and models, is a simple apparatus consisting of a bowl-like container which fits into the top of a decanter. This bowl, which is where the coffee and water are mixed together, has a felt filter pad at the bottom over a small drainage hole plugged by a rubber stopper.

Cold water extract is prepared by combining one pound of regular or perk grind coffee in the upper bowl with two quarts of cold water. The mixture should be folded rather than stirred because stirring may settle some of the finer grind at the bottom of the container and clog the filter. The mixture is allowed to sit overnight or about twelve hours. Then the plug is pulled from the bottom of the bowl so the coffee extract can filter through the felt pad into the decanter below. Although commercially made extractors work well, you can save yourself some expense by making your own extractor along the lines suggested above.

The coffee extract should be kept sealed in the

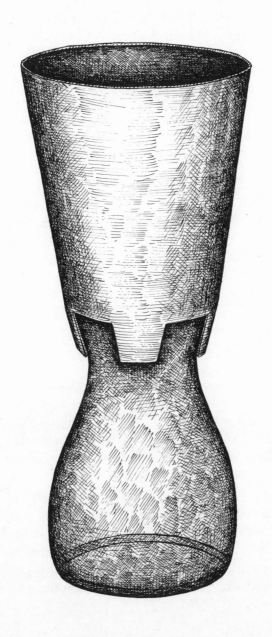

refrigerator. It can be kept for up to two weeks, but it loses optimum flavor after a few days. If you want to keep a supply of extract handy for longer periods of time, you can freeze it with no adverse effect. To make coffee from the extract, spoon an ounce or two into a cup with boiling water.

Espresso

Espresso is a dark, very strong coffee quite popular in Europe. It is made by forcing boiling water and steam through a finely ground dark roast. It requires an espresso maker and, traditionally, an espresso roast, both of which are avilable in any good coffee store. However, if espresso is too strong for you at first, you can work your way up to it by using a lighter roast in an espresso machine to produce an espressolike medium coffee. Espresso beans are easy to recognize. They are dark and completely covered with a shiny coat of oil.

The simplest home espresso maker is a two-chamber aluminum pot which makes very good espresso and is priced from about six dollars. The pot consists of a bottom chamber which holds the water, a perforated coffee basket with a short hollow stem, and a top chamber where the brewed coffee is received through a central spigot. In the preparation of espresso, the lower chamber is filled with cold water up to the pressure-escape valve, a brass fitting in the wall of the pot. The basket is filled with medium to fine espresso grind. It should not be tamped. If you like slightly thicker espresso, it is better on the whole to

get stronger espresso by using less water. If the basket is packed too tightly, the flow of water to the top chamber will be impeded (testing the effectiveness of the safety valve). After the coffee basket has been filled, the basket is placed in the lower chamber and the entire assembly is screwed together tightly. The pot is placed on medium heat and the water in the lower chamber is forced up through the coffee into the upper chamber. As soon as the upper chamber is filled with coffee, the pot should be removed from the heat and the coffee should be served. Plain espresso is usually served in a demitasse. Mixed espresso drinks are served in larger cups.

In addition to the home espresso pot just described, most coffee stores carry noncommercial espresso makers which range as high as two hundred and fifty dollars. More expensive machines are usually electric and have such features as chrome plating, pressure controls, a water-level indicator, and a steam nozzle for steaming milk. The steam nozzle is handy for making such espresso drinks as cappuccino and mocha fino (see Chapter 6).

Turkish Coffee

Like espresso, Turkish coffee is very strong. It is popular in eastern Mediterranean countries, where it plays an important part in conversation and entertainment.

For best results this beverage should be made in a Turkish coffee maker, called an *ibrik*. This is an open-top, ladle-handled pot, usually two and a half to

three inches in diameter and three to five inches deep. Arabian mocha, ground to a fine powder, is traditionally used for Turkish coffee.

In the preparation of Turkish coffee, two table-spoons of powdered coffee and one tablespoon of sugar are placed in the pot with four ounces of water per cup. This mixture is brought to a boil on medium heat until foam rises to the top of the pot. The foam is spooned into the serving cups, which are a bit smaller than a demitasse. The pot is returned to the heat until foam rises and the foam is spooned into the serving cups a second time. The coffee is heated to boiling a third time and then poured carefully down the inside walls of the serving cups. In the cups, the coffee is allowed to cool slightly and the grounds are given time to settle. The beverage is sipped, and only two-thirds of a cup is consumed. Powdered cardamom is often mixed with the coffee in this preparation.

6. BLENDS, ADDITIVES, MIXES, AND RECIPES

BLENDS AND BLENDING

After you've become acquainted with the various coffee tastes available on the gourmet market, you may want to experiment with blends, especially if you haven't found the exact taste you're looking for. Properly done, blending is the mixing together of beans that have been roasted. Once the correct proportions of the roast beans have been mixed uniformly, all or a portion of the blend is then ground for brewing. Unlike the mass market coffee business, which uses skillful blending partly to mitigate the taste of inferior beans, quality coffee blending marries the best characteristics of coffees already good enough to stand alone. Thus, if you find an especially pleasing characteristic in each of several different coffees, you may be able to enjoy all of them in a blend.

As a consumer, you have three options in the pursuit of blended coffee. You can buy one or more of the house or standard blends offered by gourmet coffee stores. You can have the store prepare a blend to your specifications. Or, you can blend your own coffee.

House blends are as varied in name and ingredients as the taste fantasies of coffee store owners, although they usually contain a high percentage of Western Hemisphere coffees. Whatever a house blend is called, its contents will usually be printed along with its name. In fact, the store may occasionally brew a fresh sample of the blend to acquaint customers with its taste. Perhaps the most famous standard blend in gourmet coffee is Mocha-Java, which combines the aroma and dry cocoa taste of Mocha with the light body in Java to produce a well-rounded coffee with the best features of each. Another standard blend in the gourmet trade is Vienna blend, which is the combination of dark and light roast beans, usually half-and-half. Vienna blend shouldn't be confused with Vienna roast, a dark roast which is slightly lighter than espresso.

Sometimes gourmet coffee drinkers discover a blend they like but prefer to avoid the labor of mixing the ingredients themselves. In such cases, the coffee store is usually happy to mix the beans and furnish the blend either in whole bean or ground form. Coffee stores frequently maintain a file of blend specifications for their regular customers so that blend purchases can be ordered and prepared in advance with a minimum of instructions. We know of a state law enforcement agency whose office personnel have settled on a blend of one part Guatemala, one part Colombia, and one part Costa Rica. Whenever they place an order, they simply ask for "the law enforcement blend," and the store personnel know precisely what beans to mix.

Some coffee drinkers like to blend their own beans. This allows them to blend smaller quantities at a time and to continue experimenting with different coffee types and proportions.

If you are interested in doing your own blending, you should keep these basic guidelines in mind:

1. Know the taste of the individual coffees before you blend them. You should have a notion of what desirable flavor characteristics you want to bring out in the blend.

2. Blend the desirable flavor characteristics of one coffee into the absence or weakness of these characteristics in other coffees.

3. Remember that dark roasts dominate light roasts when equal proportions are used.

4. If you like the taste of a number of coffees from the same region of the world, try blending some of them. Blending coffees with similar characteristics, say two mild Western Hemisphere coffees, will result in coffee that is fuller in body and rounder in flavor than either of the original ingredients.

5. Don't expect the blending of a lot of different coffees to produce a blend of any distinction. The more coffees put into a blend, the less like any particular coffee the blend will taste.

6. In judging the outcome of your blending through beverage tasting, follow the flavor changes as the coffee cools. Subtle characteristics of the blend may appear, fade, and reappear as the temperature falls. Since coffee stratifies to some extent, you should stir the beverage before you pour it.

7. Use accurate measurements in your blending experiments and keep a record of them for reference.

Chicory in Blending

Much has been made of the taste qualities of coffee blended with the roasted and ground root of chicory, a perennial flowering plant. The advertising spots of some mass market coffees have even touted chicory as an exotic ingredient which automatically makes those coffees better. The truth of the matter is that chicory is a cheap substitute for coffee. It not only costs about two-thirds as much as coffee, but its distinctive flavor helps disguise some of the disagreeable or mediocre taste characteristics of beans used in mass market blends.

Nevertheless, some people do like chicory blended in good coffee. Where it is blended with gourmet coffee, chicory is usually added to darker roasts it can't overpower. It has a tart, faintly syrupy taste, and it adds body to coffee, but it overshadows the delicate flavor and aroma of mild or medium Arabicas.

Some Blends You Might Try

As we've noted, you should blend coffees on the basis of your own taste preferences. However, in case you'd like some blending combinations to use as a point of departure, here are some you might enjoy:

> 1/2 Colombia, 1/2 Kenya
>
> 1/3 Celebes, 1/3 Colombia, 1/3 Kenya
>
> 3/8 Brazil, 3/8 Colombia, 1/4 Mocha
>
> 1/3 Java, 1/3 Mocha, 1/3 Colombia
>
> 1/3 Ethiopia, 2/3 Colombia
>
> 1/3 Celebes and 2/3 of your favorite Western Hemisphere coffee
>
> 1/4 espresso or continental roast, 3/8 Mexico, 3/8 Ethiopia
>
> 1/2 espresso roast Colombia, 1/2 Mocha
>
> 1/2 Colombia, 1/2 Kona
>
> 1/3 Tanzania and 2/3 of your favorite Western Hemisphere coffee

ADDITIVES

Sugar was first added to coffee in Cairo in the early 1600s to offset the bitterness of the beverage of that day. Things haven't changed much. The majority of Americans drink mass marketed coffee and the majority of them who use such additives as sugar and cream do so to make their coffee tolerable.

We're convinced that a lot of people used to additives in their canned, grocery store coffee wouldn't want them in a cup of good Arabica coffee. However, there's certainly nothing wrong with some additives in gourmet coffee. For example, fresh, unsterilized cream in a cup of rich Arabica coffee makes a delicious drink. Sugar is customary in espresso; and sugar, sugar diet substitutes, or honey often add a pleasing dimension to good coffee. However, the nondairy milk or cream substitutes, charitably called whiteners, are better left on a grocery store shelf along with grocery store coffee.

MIXED COFFEE DRINKS
AND COFFEE DISHES

Coffee is a fantastic mixer in the world of beverage flavors. It's especially good when flavored *by* other ingredients and served hot. But it also makes a pleasing flavor ingredient in a lot of cold drinks and cooking recipes. Following are some fairly traditional recipes for hot coffee drinks as well as some attractive cold-drink ideas and coffee-cooking recipes, compliments of the Pan-American Coffee Bureau.

Hot Drinks

CAFÉ AU LAIT

coffee
whole milk or milk with 5 percent cream

Make strong coffee. Heat the milk to scalding in a separate pan. Pour equal amounts simultaneously into each cup.

CAFÉ BORGIA

espresso
1 cup of whipping cream
vanilla extract
sugar
powdered, unsweetened chocolate
grated orange peel

Brew double-strength espresso. In a chilled bowl beat the whipping cream, adding 1/4 teaspoon of vanilla extract and one teaspoon sugar. Put 1/4 teaspoon chocolate in each serving cup. Fill cups 3/4 with espresso and stir. Place heaping tablespoon of whipped cream preparation on top of espresso. Sprinkle with grated orange peel.

CAFÉ LIQUEUR

your favorite medium- to dark-roast coffee
your favorite liqueur

Brew strong coffee. To each freshly poured cup, add a dollop of the liqueur to suit your taste.

MOCHA FINO

espresso
sugar
powdered chocolate
powdered cinnamon
whole or 5 percent milk

Brew double-strength espresso. In 8- to 10-ounce serving cups place one tablespoon sugar, 1/8 tablespoon chocolate, 1/8 tablespoon cinnamon. Add 4 ounces of espresso and stir. Fill remainder with steamed milk. Sprinkle 1/4 teaspoon chocolate on top.

CAFÉ CHOCOLATE

coffee
cocoa
milk

Make a pot of coffee. Prepare an equal amount of hot cocoa using milk, and then combine the two. Pour into serving cups and top with whipped cream.

IRISH COFFEE

coffee
whipping cream
white sugar
vanilla extract
Irish whiskey
brown sugar

Brew strong coffee. In a chilled bowl beat together cream, white sugar, and vanilla. To each 8-ounce mug (or Irish whiskey glass, if you have a set) add a jigger or so of whiskey, a tablespoon of brown sugar, and coffee. Stir. The whipped cream should be scooped up on the back of a spoon and set gently on the coffee. The flavor of this drink is enhanced by drinking the coffee *through* the cream.

CAPPUCCINO

espresso coffee
whole or 5 percent milk
unsweetened, powdered chocolate

Ideally, cappuccino should be made with an espresso maker
that has a steamer nozzle attachment. Brew the espresso.
In a narrow pan pour the milk (1/3 cup for each 2/3 cup of
espresso.) Submerge the steamer nozzle in the milk and
steam it at intervals of a few seconds each until the milk is
frothy with small bubbles. Gently lay the steamed milk
onto the espresso, in tall, slender cups if you have them.
Top with a dash of powdered chocolate.

If you don't have a milk steamer, heat milk in a pan, stirring
frequently. Don't boil. If you want to froth the hot milk,
run it through a blender at high speed.

Cold Drinks

The first iced-coffee recipe which follows is fairly uni-
versal. The remainder of the cold coffee drink ideas
come from the Pan-American Coffee Bureau. These
recipes call for strong or extra-strong coffee because
ice and other liquids in the recipes would dilute and
diminish the flavor contribution of coffee brewed at
ordinary strength.

ICED COFFEE

> extra-strong coffee
> ice
> water

Brew extra-strong coffee. Place ice in a pitcher and pour
cold water over it at a ratio of two cups of water and ice per
cup of strong coffee. Pour the fresh hot coffee into the ice
water. Keep in refrigerator and serve over ice.

SPICED ICED COFFEE

8 cups coffee
1 whole cinnamon stick
8 whole cloves
sugar to taste
cream

Brew 8 cups of coffee using 1½ measures of coffee per cup. When coffee is brewed, add cinnamon and cloves. Allow to cool, then refrigerate until chilled. Put ice cubes in tall glasses and strain coffee over the ice. Pour cream into the coffee just before serving. Serve with sugar. Serves 6.

MOCHA FROSTED

2½ cups cold strong coffee
5 tablespoons chocolate
2 cups vanilla ice cream

Place all ingredients in bowl and beat with rotary beater or wire whip until smooth. Pour into tall glasses. Serves 4.

CAFÉ CHOCOMALT

1 cup cold strong coffee
1 cup milk
1 cup chocolate ice cream
2 tablespoons sugar
3 tablespoons malted-milk powder

Mix all ingredients in blender at high speed. Serve in tall glasses. Serves 2.

CAFÉ SEVILLE

cold extra-strong coffee
crushed or chopped ice
2 tablespoons sugar
1/4 cup Cointreau or Grand Marnier
1/4 teaspoon grated orange rind
1 cup milk

Put ice in cup to half-cup level, then fill to top with coffee. Combine with remaining ingredients in blender and whip at high speed until foamy. Serve in tall glasses, garnished with orange slice. Serves 2.

BANANA SHAKE

1½ cups cold strong coffee
3 tablespoons sugar
1 banana
1 cup vanilla ice cream

Cut banana in chunks and combine with coffee and sugar in blender at high speed. When mixture is smooth, add ice cream and blend at medium speed until smooth. Serves 2.

PEANUT BUTTER CAFÉ

1 cup cold strong coffee
1 cup milk
1 heaping tablespoon peanut butter
4 tablespoons sugar

Mix in blender at high speed until foamy. Serve in tall glasses. Serves 2.

CAFÉ VINO

1 cup cold strong coffee
2 ounces Tawny Port or Muscatel wine
2 tablespoons sugar
1/2 teaspoon grated orange peel
dash of cinnamon

Whip in blender at high speed until foamy. Pour into chilled wine glasses. Serves 2.

COGNACKAFFEE

3 eggs, chilled
grated peel of 1/2 lemon
1/4 cup sugar
1½ cups cold strong coffee
1/3 cup cognac or brandy

Break eggs into blender, add grated lemon and beat until fluffy. Add sugar and beat until thick. Add coffee, then cognac. Serve in brandy snifters. Serves 4.

CAFÉ HAWAIIAN

2 cups cold strong coffee
1 cup chilled pineapple juice
2 tablespoons sugar
2 cups coffee ice cream

Combine ingredients and beat with rotary beater or mix in blender until smooth and foamy. Pour into tall glasses. Serves 4.

CAFÉ MOCHA MINT

    1 cup cold strong coffee
    1 cup chocolate ice cream
    2 ounces crème de menthe

Mix all ingredients in blender at low speed. Serve in champagne or wine glasses. Serves 4.

Coffee Cooking

    As a cooking ingredient, coffee makes its flavors most apparent in pastries and desserts. Therefore, we're first listing some tantalizing pastry and dessert recipes. Because we've borrowed the recipes, we haven't tampered with them, but where they call for instant coffee powder, we recommend that you use freeze-dried instant. As a type, it is more flavorful than regular instants, and it is more soluble in cold mixes.

    In the main course recipes we've listed, you probably won't taste the coffee per se, but its presence will enhance the overall flavors of each dish.

Pastries

COFFEE CREAM HORNS

    1/2 pound butter or margarine well chilled, divided
    2 cups plus 2 tablespoons sifted all-purpose flour
    1/2 cup ice water
    1 tablespoon lemon juice
    12 foil-wrapped ice cream cones
    1 egg slightly beaten
    Coffee Almond Cream*

Cut 1/4 pound butter into flour until mixture resembles cornmeal. Add water and lemon juice all at once. Stir with fork until pastry stays together. Cover; chill 1/2 hour. Roll out 1/4-inch thick into rectangle 18 x 12 inches. Cut remaining butter into thin pats; cover 2/3 rectangle. Fold uncovered third over middle third; fold opposite end over top. Then fold pastry in thirds crosswise to form a block. Roll out again 1/4-inch thick. Repeat folding. Wrap in foil. Chill 1/2 hour. Repeat rolling, folding, and chilling three more times. Wrap pastry. Chill overnight, or longer. Roll pastry 1/8-inch thick into rectangle 20 x 12 inches. Cut into 12 inch-wide strips. Brush with water. Wrap each strip, slightly overlapping, around foil-covered cone, starting at point. Brush with egg, chill 1/2 hour. Bake at 450° for 15 minutes. Reduce heat to 350°. Bake 15 minutes or until puffed and golden. Cool on racks. Remove cones carefully. Before serving, fill with Coffee Almond Cream.*

*Coffee Almond Cream

Combine 1/2 cup whipping cream, 2 tablespoons sugar, and 1 tablespoon instant coffee. Chill. Whip until stiff. Fold.in 1/3 cup diced roasted almonds.

COFFEE ALMOND DATE LOAF

2 cups sifted all-purpose flour
4 teaspoons baking powder
1 teaspoon salt
2/3 cup sugar
1/3 cup chopped blanched almonds
3/4 cup finely cut, pitted dates
1/4 cup minced candied ginger
1 cup strong coffee
1/8 teaspoon baking soda
1 egg, well beaten
2 tablespoons melted shortening

Mix and sift flour, baking powder, salt, and sugar. Stir in almonds, dates, and candied ginger. Combine coffee, baking soda, and shortening. Add all at once to dry ingredients. Stir only enough to dampen dry ingredients. Turn into greased loaf pan, 8 x 5 x 2 inches, or a straight-sided loaf pan, 4½ x 11¼ x 5¾ inches. Let stand 20 minutes. Bake at 375° about 45 minutes.

COFFEE BANANA PIE

    1 envelope unflavored gelatine
    1/4 cup cold water
    1 package vanilla pudding mix
       (regular, not instant)
    1 cup strong coffee
    1/2 cup milk
    2 medium bananas
    1 teaspoon lemon juice
    1 teaspoon sugar
    1 teaspoon rum flavoring
    1 cup whipping cream, divided
    1 package lady fingers

Soften gelatine in cold water. Dissolve over hot water. Prepare pudding mix as directed on package, using coffee and milk as the liquid. Add dissolved gelatine to hot pudding; mix well. Put one banana, lemon juice, and sugar in electric blender or food mill. Blend until liquefied (about 1/2 cup). Add to pudding mixture with rum flavoring. Chill thoroughly. Beat until bubbly. Whip 1/2 cup cream and fold in. Line bottom of 9-inch pie pan with split lady fingers. Make a rim of split lady fingers around edge. Spoon filling carefully into pie pan. Chill until firm. Garnish with fluted slices from remaining banana and remaining cream, whipped.

Desserts

COFFEE FROZEN CUSTARD

3/4 cup sugar
1 tablespoon instant coffee
dash of salt
1/2 cup water
1/4 cup light corn syrup
2 envelopes unflavored gelatine
1/2 cup cold water
2 cups instant nonfat dry milk crystals
1 quart whole milk
1 teaspoon vanilla or 1/2 teaspoon brandy flavoring

Make coffee syrup by mixing together sugar, instant coffee, salt, 1/2 cup water, and corn syrup in saucepan. Bring to a boil and boil 2 minutes. In a cup, sprinkle gelatine over 1/2 cup cold water to soften. Stir instant crystals into whole milk; blend in softened gelatine and hot coffee syrup. Cook over low heat, stirring constantly, until gelatine dissolves. Remove from heat. Stir in flavoring. Turn into refrigerator trays and freeze until firm. Beat until smooth. Spoon into sherbet or parfait glasses, or pipe through pastry tube. Makes 8 to 10 servings.

MOCHA POT-DE-CRÉME

1½ cups whipping cream
1/2 cup strong coffee
6 ounces grated sweet cooking chocolate
2 tablespoons sugar
6 egg yolks, slightly beaten
1 teaspoon vanilla

Combine cream, coffee, chocolate, and sugar. Cook and stir over very low heat until chocolate melts and cream is scalded. Remove from heat. Pour a little of the hot mixture

on egg yolks. Blend. Return to remaining hot mixture. Add
vanilla. Mix well. Strain into pots-de-crème or custard
cups. Cover. (If custard cups are used, cover with foil.) Set
in pan of warm water. Bake in preheated 300° oven for 20
minutes. Chill. Makes 6 servings.

CLASSIC COFFEE MOUSSE

> 3 envelopes unflavored gelatine
> 2/3 cup sugar
> 2½ tablespoons cornstarch
> 2 cups milk
> 8 eggs, well beaten
> 4 tablespoons instant coffee powder
> 3/4 cup water
> 2 cups whipping cream

Mix gelatine, sugar, and cornstarch in 2½-quart saucepan.
Stir in milk. Stir constantly over medium heat until gelatine
dissolves and mixture thickens and comes to a boil. Remove
from heat. Gradually stir hot mixture into beaten eggs (a
wire whisk works well for this). Return mixture to saucepan. Stir constantly over low heat 2 minutes. Strain immediately into large bowl. Chill, stirring frequently, until
mixture is thoroughly cool. Dissolve instant coffee in water.
Stir into gelatine mixture. Chill, stirring frequently, until
slightly thickened. Whip cream; fold in. Turn into 2-quart
mold; chill until firm. Unmold. Makes 12 servings. Serve
with Coffee-Vanilla Sauce.*

*Coffee-Vanilla Sauce

Combine 1/2 cup sugar, 1½ tablespoons cornstarch, and
1/4 teaspoon salt in saucepan. Mix well. Add 2 cups boiling
water slowly, while stirring. Bring to boil. Boil 5 minutes.
Add 2 teaspoons vanilla and 1/4 cup coffee liqueur. Chill.
Makes 8 servings.

Main Dishes

CHICKEN PAPRIKA

1 frying chicken (2 to 3 pounds), disjointed
  giblets
1 small onion
3 or 4 parsley sprigs
2 teaspoons salt, divided
4 peppercorns
1 bay leaf
1/4 cup finely chopped onions
4 tablespoons fat, divided
1 cup flour, divided
6 teaspoons paprika, divided
1/3 cup cream
1/3 cup strong coffee
1½ cups thick sour cream

Place giblets in saucepan with 2 cups water, 1 small onion, parsley, 1 teaspoon salt, peppercorns, and bay leaf. Cover; simmer 1 hour. Cook chopped onion in 2 tablespoons fat until soft but not brown. Remove onion and reserve, leaving fat in skillet. Combine flour (all but 2 tablespoons), 1 teaspoon salt, and 2 teaspoons paprika in paper bag. Shake chicken pieces until coated. Brown well in fat. Add 2 tablespoons giblet broth. Cook chicken, covered, slowly 35 to 40 minutes or until tender. In saucepan, melt 2 tablespoons fat. Blend in 2 tablespoons flour. Add 1 cup giblet broth, cream, coffee, and 4 teaspoons paprika. Stir over low heat until smooth and thickened.

Return chopped onion to pan. Add sour cream gradually, stirring vigorously. Pour sauce over chicken in skillet; cook over low heat 3 minutes, turning chicken and stirring sauce. Do not boil. Makes 4 servings.

IRISH-AMERICAN STEW

3 pounds boned lean lamb
1/4 cup vegetable oil
2 cans (1 pound each) small white onions
water
1 cup tomato juice
1 cup strong coffee
2 teaspoons salt
1/8 teaspoon pepper
1/2 teaspoon sugar
1 small yellow turnip
2 packages (10 ounces each) frozen asparagus cuts
1 package biscuit mix
2 tablespoons parsley
1/3 cup flour
1/2 cup cold water

Cut lamb in 2-inch chunks; brown in hot oil. Pour off excess oil. Measure liquid from canned onions and add enough water to make 4 cups. Add with tomato juice, coffee, and seasonings. Simmer 2½ hours, or until meat is tender. Pare turnip. Cut in 1-inch chunks; add to meat. Simmer 1/2 hour. Add onions and asparagus. Simmer 10 minutes longer. Make small dumplings with biscuit mix according to package directions, adding 2 tablespoons minced parsley. Cook in stew as directed. Remove dumplings. Keep warm. Blend flour and water. Add to hot stew. Stir until gravy thickens. Serve stew topped with dumplings. Makes 8 servings.

VENETIAN VEAL

8 slices bacon
3/4 cup chopped onion
3 garlic cloves, slashed
1½ pounds veal, thinly sliced (as for veal scaloppine)
salt, pepper, paprika
1 can or package chicken noodle soup mix
1 cup canned Italian plum tomatoes
1 can (3 ounces) sliced broiled mushrooms
1 teaspoon Worcestershire sauce
1/2 cup strong coffee
1 tablespoon cornstarch
2 tablespoons cold water
1/2 cup Sauterne

Fry bacon crisp. Drain. Cook onion and garlic in drippings until lightly browned. Discard garlic. Remove onion and reserve. Brown veal in drippings. Remove. Sprinkle veal with salt, pepper, and paprika to taste. Prepare soup mix as directed, but use only 2 cups of water. Simmer 7 minutes. Add tomatoes, mushrooms with their broth, Worcestershire sauce, coffee, and soup to drippings. Blend cornstarch and cold water. Add and stir until thickened. Return bacon, veal, and onion to pan. Simmer 30 minutes. Stir in Sauterne. Serve over rice with water chestnuts. Makes 6 servings.

BEEF BOURGUIGNON

    4 tablespoons butter or margarine
    3 pounds round steak, cut in 3/4-inch cubes
    1 clove garlic, crushed
    3 onions, sliced
    4 tablespoons flour
    2 cups Burgundy
    1 cup water
    2 teaspoons salt
    1/2 teaspoon monosodium glutamate
    1/2 teaspoon pepper
    1/4 teaspoon marjoram
    1/4 teaspoon oregano
    1/2 cup strong coffee

Melt butter or margarine in deep frying pan or chicken fryer. Add cubed round steak. Brown on all sides. Add garlic and onions. Cook until onions are soft but not brown. Remove meat and onions from pan. Blend flour with butter remaining in kettle. Add wine, water, seasonings, and coffee. Stir until slightly thickened. Return meat and onions to kettle. Cover. Bring to boil. Simmer 1½ hours or until meat is tender. Serve with parslied, buttered broad noodles. Makes 6 servings.

7.
COFFEE
AND YOUR
BODY

Voltaire, who drank coffee all his life, was reportedly involved in a long and tedious conversation one day with a woman who droned on and on that coffee was harmful to people's health. "It's an insidious and slow poison," the lady declared knowingly.

"Indeed, it must be a slow poison," agreed Voltaire, "for I am eighty-four and not dead yet."

The issue of whether or not coffee is injurious to health has been debated for hundreds of years, beginning shortly after the beverage was discovered. In 1511, coffee was publicly condemned in Mecca by Islamic religious leaders who declared its use contrary to the teachings of Islam and harmful to body and soul. Their declaration was heeded in Cairo, where coffee warehouses were burned to the ground and coffee merchants stoned by the people. However, in 1524, Sultan Selim I reversed the decree of the wise men, declaring the drinking of coffee to be perfectly orthodox. To underscore his decision, the sultan ordered the execution of two Persian doctors who had taken the position that coffee was harmful. Thereafter, little more about the evil effects was heard in the Moslem world. The drink, in fact, became an important part of Moslem life.

When coffee drinking became popular in Europe in the seventeenth and eighteenth centuries, the allegation that it was harmful surfaced again. The controversy was partly a reflection of genuine medical and scientific concern and partly a smokescreen for other complaints against the coffee trade and the coffeehouses that served as its outlet. In the early part of the period, tavernkeepers were jealous of the competition posed by the coffeehouses. Later, as the coffeehouses became important meeting places for the exchange of ideas, including antiestablishment views, government officials began to frown on the coffee trade. In the seventeenth century a group of English wives issued a manifesto that railed against coffee and the coffeehouses as the cause of sexual impotence and domestic neglect among their husbands. In the eighteenth century there was a curious correlation between balance-of-trade deficits to coffee-producing regions and official criticism of coffee's bodily effects.

About that time tea imports were rising in Europe and the issue took on a new dimension. Scientists began to ask which was more harmful, coffee or tea?

King Gustav III of Sweden, in an effort to clarify this scientific debate, decided to use coffee and tea to execute two criminals who had been sentenced to death. One was given a large amount of strong coffee to drink every day while the other was obliged to drink an equal volume of strong tea. A committee of doctors was assigned to keep the doomed men under constant observation and inform the king of progress in the execution. To the disenchantment of eighteenth-century science, the prisoners lived to a ripe old age, surviving all of the doctors who had been assigned to the execution.

Current Findings on Coffee's Effects

Because coffee is such a popular beverage, and because it has drug properties, it continues to interest medical researchers. However, numerous studies on the bodily effects of coffee have led to the publication of conflicting conclusions, with most researchers reporting no significant evidence that coffee is harmful to health.

The researchers all do agree that coffee has a definite physiological impact on the normal, healthy adult—primarily a stimulus effect. If it didn't, it probably wouldn't be consumed as much as it is: three times more than soft drinks, four times more than beer, and fifty times more than hard liquor. Researchers also agree that tolerance to coffee seems to vary with the physiology of the individual consumer. Some people are noticeably affected by one or two cups, while others can drink much more without feeling any effects. Some people, for particular medical reasons, should not drink coffee. These are primarily people under the care of a doctor for known heart or stomach disorders. Some medical authorities have advised against giving children coffee because they feel children are more susceptible to nervous excitement from caffeine. Yet coffee is routine in the diet of children in many other cultures, and some authorities have suggested that it has a calming effect on hyperactive children which may make its use a desirable alternative to giving them amphetamines.

Before discussing some of the effects of coffee, we should point out that the beverage has virtually no nutritional value. At most, one cup provides about five calories and 10 percent of the adult daily requirement of niacin. This makes coffee a poor substitute for food, especially in the morning. Coffee's only food value is in whole bean form, which consists of about 14 percent protein. The ancient Abyssinians found that coffee beans pressed into balls of fat about the size of a peach made a good daily food ration on long journeys. A similar food is eaten in some parts of Africa today.

Coffee and Heart Disease

In the past two decades a number of population studies have been undertaken to see if there is any statistically significant relationship between coffee drinking and the onset of heart disease. Most of these studies have concluded that there is no significant correlation between the two. However, two studies show enough of a correlation to keep the question open.

The most comprehensive study showing no meaningful connection between coffee drinking and heart disease has been the Framingham (Mass.) Study, which began about 1950 and was still in effect in 1974. Basically, the Framingham Study looked for correlations between living habits and the development of cardiovascular disease in a population of roughly 5,000 people over a period of 18 years. Information on that population's coffee-drinking habits, gathered over a 12-year period, showed no significant relationship between coffee drinking and the onset of heart disease among people with no history of heart trouble. A significant correlation was found between coffee consumption and death from all causes in the male population, but the researchers concluded that this correlation existed only because of the high percentage of male smokers who also drank coffee. Cigarette smoking, high blood pressure, and high serum cholesterol levels were the most important risk factor associated with heart disease by Framingham researchers. Another study showing essentially negative connections between coffee drinking and heart disease was the Kaiser-Permanente Study of 464 subjects between 1964 and 1970.

The two studies showing a correlation between coffee drinking and heart disease were the Western Electric Study, conducted in the Chicago area from 1957 through the late 1960s, and the Boston Collaborative Drug Surveillance Program in the early 1970s. The Chicago study, which surveyed the coffee-drinking habits of more than 1,000 men, found less heart disease among men drinking up to three cups a day than among noncoffee drinkers. But it found more heart disease among men drinking five cups a day than among moderate or noncoffee drinkers. Curiously, the heart disease death rate was highest among men who drank no coffee and men who drank more than five cups a day. The Boston study found a higher incidence of coffee consumption among patients who had been hospitalized for heart attack.

We haven't the space to get into a detailed analysis of these studies, but we do have several general reactions. First, studies like Framingham and Kaiser-Permanente seem more valid in regard to a general coffee-drinking public because they began with a homogeneous selection of relatively healthy subjects and took into account most of the variables which might be associated with heart disease. The Boston study, on the other hand, used ailing subjects and did not take into account their diet other than coffee. It isn't surprising that researchers in the Western Electric and Boston studies disclaim any causal connection between the incidence of coffee drinking and heart disease. Second, we agree that the existence of research correlations between coffee drinking and heart disease, despite their confounding variables or limitations in data, indicate that more study is needed. Third, we're not sure how applicable any of these studies are to the kind of coffee discussed in this book. The medical research is either ignorant of or insensitive to differences in coffee quality. Since at least 95 percent of the coffee consumed in the United States is mass market coffee, it is probable that most of the coffee referred to in the research was the mass market type. Yet we're convinced that specialty or gourmet coffee is very different not only in taste but in its physiological impact. As we'll discuss below, specialty coffee contains much less caffeine than mass market coffee, and it doesn't cause the gastric distress that mass market coffee often does. It seems that,

further research on coffee and health should take into
account differences in coffee quality and character.
Just as all cooking oils are not the same, so all coffees
are not the same.

Caffeine and Some of Its Effects

Because it produces the most noticeable effects, caffeine seems to be the most significant chemical agent
in coffee. Although it is present in a number of other
foods, it is named after coffee and has been popularly
associated with the beverage since it was isolated by a
chemist in 1820. However, coffee has many active
ingredients besides caffeine. These ingredients,
mainly roasting by-products, also affect bodily func-
tions. However, because coffee research has focused
primarily on caffeine, much less is known about the
specific influences of roasting by-products.

An average five-ounce serving of mass market coffee contains between 90 and 125 milligrams of caffeine, while premium Arabica coffees have a significantly lower caffeine level. By comparison, an equal
amount of tea, depending upon the type, contains between 30 and 70 milligrams. Most cola soft drinks
contain about 37 milligrams per five-ounce serving.
Nonprescription caffeine alkaloid stimulants sold in
drug and grocery stores contain between 100 and 200
milligrams per pill.

Caffeine principally affects the brain, the cardiovascular system, and the kidneys. It also increases
breathing and metabolism.

Coffee's influence in the brain results mainly from the stimulating effects of caffeine on the cerebral cortex. Research indicates that these effects include a speeding up of thought processes, an increase in the association of ideas, a sense of euphoria, and an increased ability to memorize simple numbers, concepts, and thought sequences. While caffeine is the dominant cause of these reactions, research suggests that some of the other ingredients in coffee play a part in stimulating the central nervous system.

Coffee's effects on the cardiovascular system, which seem to result from caffeine, are somewhat more complex. What could be considered a moderate intake of coffee, perhaps one or two cups several times during a day, will produce little effect on the heart and blood vessels of most people. Larger intakes of coffee, say three or four cups several times during the day, will put enough caffeine into the system to slow the pulse rate somewhat, contract peripheral blood vessels, and raise the blood pressure. In addition, it will dilate blood vessels of the kidneys, muscles, skin, and heart, and cause the heart to contract a bit harder in its pumping function. Excessive drinking of coffee containing caffeine will sometimes cause irregular heart beats or palpitations. However, these symptoms disappear and leave no apparent aftereffects following a decrease in coffee consumption.

The other principal effect of caffeine in coffee is a stimulation of the kidneys to greater urine output. Because of this diuretic effect, coffee was once prescribed for this purpose by doctors. However, more effective diuretics have since been found.

Tolerance to caffeine varies from person to person, so you'll have to determine your own level of caffeine intake in your coffee drinking. However, if you want to enjoy coffee without caffeine, you don't have to buy mass market decaffeinated coffee (which is generally as bad as regular mass market coffee). Most coffee specialty stores carry decaffeinated whole bean coffee, often Columbia or one of the other Western Hemisphere Arabicas. These have about 3.3 milligrams of caffeine per cup. Of course, simply drinking Arabica coffee involves a significantly smaller intake of caffeine. Robusta beans, which are blended into most mass market coffees, have about twice the caffeine content of Arabica beans. Another way to avoid higher levels of caffeine in coffee is to avoid drinking perked coffee. Perking extracts about 10 percent more caffeine from ground coffee than drip brewing.

If you drink good Arabica coffee in moderation, you shouldn't have to buy decaffeinated beans. Even Arabica in decaffeinated form has its drawbacks. First, because coffee stores typically offer only one kind of decaffeinated beans, your choice of coffee tastes is limited to what's available. Second, decaffeinated beans are invariably roasted quite dark in order to disguise the subtle change of flavor resulting from decaffeination. Green coffee beans are decaffeinated by one of two basic methods. Decaffeination of gourmet coffee beans involves putting the beans in a flow of steam which absorbs and carries off the caffeine. Mass market decaffeination usually is accomplished by soaking the beans in a chemical compound that absorbs the caffeine and then is rinsed from the beans.

If you do overdo your coffee intake on occasion and get jittery or feel heart palpitations, the best thing to do is stop for a while and give some thought to moderation. The pleasure of good coffee, like most worthwhile things, is ruined by overindulgence.

Other Effects of Coffee

Coffee has a number of effects related more to by-products of roasting than to caffeine. The most notable of these are a laxative influence and stimulation of the stomach to greater secretion of acid.

We've heard a number of people complain that they can't drink coffee because it gives them a "sour" or acid stomach. Without exception, however, further questioning revealed that the coffee which produced these effects was mass market or vending machine coffee. These coffees are sour tasting to begin with. But, in addition, they can stimulate a 400 percent increase in secretion of stomach acid, leaving the consumer with a queasy stomach and a case of heartburn. At least one large concern has mass marketed a coffee treated to avoid causing acid stomach. Unfortunately, we can't commend its taste. Arabica coffees also cause an increase in stomach-acid secretion, but not noticeably and uncomfortably like cheaper blends of mass market coffees, and particularly not like instant coffees.

Coffee and Sleep

Although coffee can speed up your mental faculties and help you get moving after you've had some rest, there's no certainty that it will keep you from sleeping under normal bedtime circumstances or that it will keep you awake if you are trying to stay up while your body is crying for rest. We know people who can drink several cups of coffee before bedtime and sleep with no trouble at all. Others claim that coffee before bedtime will keep them from falling asleep for quite some time.

Coffee has contradictory effects when it comes to sleep. While it can stimulate the kind of mental alertness and thought activity that may make it difficult to fall asleep, it also can create a sense of well-being that brings on relaxation and sleep. The result seems to depend on which effect a person's body succumbs to most readily. Of course, other factors besides coffee influence sleepiness—room temperature, the person's emotional state, what and how much the person had to eat. Even the person's expectations about coffee's influence on sleep can be a factor. In one study where the subjects drank both regular and decaffeinated coffee but didn't know the true nature of the coffee, they reported trouble falling asleep if the coffee was labeled "regular" and ease of falling asleep if the coffee was labeled "decaffeinated."

A Final Word on Coffee and Health

Because there is much research yet to be done on coffee and health, it's not likely that this controversy, hundreds of years old, will be resolved in the near future.

But until more is known, we would like to offer

this advice: Pay attention to your body; and if you have any special trouble with coffee, see your doctor. As we've noted, coffee affects each individual differently. Your body and your doctor will tell you more about coffee's effects on your own system than any general account you might hear or read.

8.
COFFEE FROM BUSH TO BAG

As a consumer, you can control the quality of your cup of coffee through the kinds of whole bean or ground coffee you buy, and through the way you prepare it. However, what happens to coffee before it reaches the roaster determines what retail options you have.

This chapter briefly discusses the cultivation and processing of coffee. Most important, it points out some basic differences in handling that have a lot to do with the way coffee tastes in your cup. Although we don't try to present an in-depth technical study of coffee cultivation or processing, we outline enough of this part of the coffee trade to give you a basic idea of what happens to green coffee before it becomes a roast.

COFFEE ON THE BUSH

There are about 100 different kinds of coffee plants known today, but as we noted earlier, only two varieties have any significant commercial value—Arabica and Robusta, which account for 99 percent of world coffee production.

Coffee bushes or trees are cultivated principally in the torrid zone between the tropics of Cancer and Capricorn. They grow at a variety of altitudes, but the most favorable conditions exist at elevations between 3,000 and 6,000 feet above sea level. Coffee grows in a variety of soils, but produces better-tasting fruit when raised in mountainous volcanic soils containing rich deposits of nitrogen, phosphorus, potash, other trace mineral elements, and humus from decayed vegetation.

A new coffee tree will bear its first fruit in five to eight years. Its productive life span averages between twenty-five and thirty-five years. Producing trees yield about five pounds of coffee cherries each year, but because it takes roughly five pounds of coffee cherries to produce one pound of clean green beans, each tree actually yields about a pound of green coffee annually.

What we commonly call the coffee bean is actually the dried seed of the coffee cherry. These cherries, which turn ruby-red or purple when ripe, grow in clusters on the plant. Inside the smooth skin of each cherry is a mushy, saccharine pulp, and within the pulp are two oblong seeds, or beans, lying against one another on their flat sides. Each bean is covered by a thin parchment, and inside that, an even thinner silvery skin.

GREEN COFFEE PROCESSING

Although good coffee flavor begins with the quality of the plant and the growing conditions, processing is critical because it can keep good coffees good and make any coffee worse. Green coffee-bean processing includes harvesting, cleaning, grading, and shipping.

Because of manual labor costs, harvesting is the most expensive part of coffee processing. The influence of labor costs has led to variations in harvesting methods that all produce a different but very definite impact on coffee quality. Arabica coffees are generally more expensive to harvest because their cherries fall to the ground soon after they ripen. This means that they must be harvested in a very short time with a large labor force. Robusta cherries, on the other hand, cling to the fruit branches after ripening. Thus, a smaller labor force can take more time to harvest a Robusta crop, allowing a grower to retain a small group of the most efficient laborers for harvesting.

Ripe coffee cherries are harvested in three general ways. They may be shaken or beaten off a tree onto the ground or large mats. Whole tree yields may simply be stripped off the branches by laborers in one picking. Or, only perfectly ripe cherries may be hand-picked by workers who return to the same plant several times as cherries mature until it has been completely picked.

The first two methods save growers a considerable amount of labor costs, but the result is a large percentage of immature and overripe cherries that produce poor coffee taste. The latter method is preferred by growers who pride themselves in the production of premium Arabica coffees. Among the producers which employ selective picking of Arabica cherries are Colombia, Costa Rica, Guatemala, Haiti, Hawaii, Kenya, and Tanganyika.

After harvesting, coffee beans must be separated from the cherry pulp, parchment, and silver skin which enclose them. There are basically two methods for doing this: dry preparation and wet preparation. Both methods influence the flavor of coffee beans.

The oldest method, and the one most commonly employed today for both Robusta and Arabica coffees, is the dry or East Indies preparation. The dry preparation consists of allowing harvested beans to lie on large drying surfaces where moisture evaporates from the cherry until it becomes a hard dry husk around the bean. The husk is then removed from the bean by hand or machine methods which break it so that it falls away from the bean and can be blown or washed away with other debris. The most significant characteristic of this hulling method is that fermentation takes place as the cherry pulp gradually dries. Since the parchment and silver skin around the bean are soluble, the flavor of the bean is affected by the fermenting pulp juices.

Many coffee experts feel that the fermentation

process improves the taste of Robusta beans, giving them a more neutral or slightly sweet flavor. However, opinion is divided on whether fermentation from dry preparation helps or damages Arabica beans. Those who prefer a delicate flavor and fragrant aroma in Arabica coffee feel that the wet process should be used. However, those who favor a stronger, tangier flavor prefer dry preparation. Brazil's Santos and Rio Arabicas have this distinctive characteristic from dry processing. Nearly all of Brazil's Arabica crop is prepared dry, partly because of tradition, partly because of the need to maintain an established taste market, and partly because the country lacks the water and labor to invest in the alternative wet preparation method.

Wet or West Indies preparation was first used as a curing method in Java but was adopted in the West Indies as an answer to the humid, rainy climate that made dry preparation difficult. In wet preparation, harvested cherries are washed and then sent through a pulping machine. This squeezes the beans out of the cherry, leaving a slime-coated bean. These beans are put into tanks for about twenty-four hours during which time enzyme fermentation breaks down the slime so it can be washed away in water. Properly controlled, this fermentation also imparts a subtle acidy taste characteristic desirable in some coffee. During this washing, beans of various densities float to different water levels. The densest beans, which sink to the bottom, are the highest quality of the batch. After washing and weight separation, the beans are spread out to dry.

After the beans have been air- or forced-air dried to what is called a glasslike hardness, they are machine-hulled to remove their parchment and silver skin. The naked beans, which have a gray-green color, are then polished by tumbling in metal cylinders. Further machine processing separates them by size and weight. If additional sorting takes place to eliminate beans that are broken, blemished, or uneven in color, it is usually done by hand.

Next, green beans are put into bags holding between 130 to 150 pounds. The bags are marked for date, type of beans, and bean grade. Coffee is graded by imperfections. The more imperfections in a random sample of beans from each bag, the lower the grade of the entire bag. Of course, a higher grade brings a higher price.

Finally, the bags are stacked on pallets and shipped to foreign markets. Green coffee is imported into North America at Quebec, New York City, New Orleans, Los Angeles, San Francisco, and Vancouver, B. C. Most of the imported coffee is purchased by mass market coffee concerns. Premium Arabicas are purchased for distribution to the small whole bean coffee stores which serve the growing gourmet coffee market.

Beyond that, the rewards of good coffee rest with you. Choose it well, brew it right, enjoy it in health.